ANTYAYORDASAKEPI

VEDIC MATHEMATICS VOLUME 1

GAURAV RAWAL

dedicated

to

my loved ones

2

Inspiration

inspired from respected
Mr Shyam Sundar Pathak sir
assistant commissioner(GST department), greater
noida

Foreword

My views to vedic maths?

The word 'veda' has this derivational meaning. It means the foundation head and illimitable store house of knowledge. This derivation means that Vedas contain all the knowledge needed by mankind for their spiritual as well as their secular, temporal and worldly aspects. To best of my knowledge I would say that every solution to any problem of human life can be solved via practical science and this all is being written in the mandals of Vedas. I would suggest my reader to go through Vedas and apply them in daily life for the achievement of all-shperes of life. The study of this aspect of my has no limits.

Forward

वैदिकगणितकेबारेमेंमेरेविचार?

‘वेद’ शब्द का यह व्युत्पन्न अर्थ है। इसका अर्थ है आधारशिला और ज्ञान का अथाह भण्डार। इस व्युत्पत्ति का अर्थ है कि वेदों में वे सभी ज्ञान समाहित हैं जिनकी मानव जाति को उनके आध्यात्मिक और साथ ही उनके लौकिक, लौकिक और सांसारिक पहलुओं के लिए आवश्यकता है। जहाँ तक मेरी जानकारी है, मैं यही कहूँगा कि मानव जीवन की किसी भी समस्या का हर समाधान व्यावहारिक विज्ञान के माध्यम से हल किया जा सकता है और यह सब वेद मंडलों में लिखा जा रहा है। मैं अपने पाठक को सुझाव दूंगा कि वे वेदों का अध्ययन करें और जीवन के सभी क्षेत्रों की उपलब्धि के लिए उन्हें दैनिक जीवन में लागू करें। मेरे इस पहलू के अध्ययन की कोई सीमा नहीं है।

Preface

Why I wrote this book

Gaurav Rawal. Yes its me the author of this book. This book is either the work of my fiction or may be it is the reality of our history. I know you all are getting confused with the fact that I am not telling you clearly that is this work fiction or realistic. But you must noted the fact that through this novel I will let your overcome your biggest fear of study that is mathematics.

In this book, I will let all my readers discover their soul and there impact on society. They will come across several suspense, thrills, and most important mathematics for our vedic age(vedic mathematics.

Several books says that there is no inscription of mathematics in Vedas, and vedic mathematics is the set of rules design by modern methods to fasten the day to calculation but I concluded that our rigvedas inscription are true and mathematics is easy to understand by knowing oneself.

You know what I am writing this book not because I want to be the writer or author. This is because my destiny is designed so. I know this work of mine is being the best seller in the world, but for its of no use because I know my destiny, I crease to exit before my final draft was printed. I was not able enjoy my victory. This is not for the reason that I am medically ill or something. The fact is before several of the gurus teaches this orally and physically but their write up can be finished. They all died by different means. I know this is my destiny and I will accept it as it is.

Preface

मैंने यह किताब क्यों लिखी

गौरव रावल। हाँ मैं ही इस पुस्तक का लेखक हूँ यह पुस्तक या तो मेरी कल्पना का काम है या हो सकता है कि यह हमारे इतिहास की वास्तविकता हो। मैं जानता हूँ कि आप सभी इस बात से भ्रमित हो रहे हैं कि मैं आपको स्पष्ट रूप से यह नहीं बता रहा हूँ कि यह कृति काल्पनिक है या यथार्थवादी। लेकिन आपको इस तथ्य पर ध्यान देना चाहिए कि इस उपन्यास के माध्यम से मैं आपके अध्ययन के सबसे बड़े डर यानी गणित को दूर कर दूंगा।

इस पुस्तक में, मैं अपने सभी पाठकों को उनकी आत्मा और समाज पर उनके प्रभाव की खोज करने दूँगा। वे हमारे वैदिक युग (वैदिक गणित) के लिए कई रहस्य, रोमांच और सबसे महत्वपूर्ण गणित लेकर आएंगे।

कई किताबें कहती हैं कि वेदों में गणित का कोई शिलालेख नहीं है, और वैदिक गणित आधुनिक तरीकों से गणना करने के लिए दिन को तेज करने के लिए डिजाइन किए गए नियमों का सेट है लेकिन मैंने निष्कर्ष निकाला कि हमारे ऋग्वेद के शिलालेख सत्य हैं और गणित को स्वयं को जानकर समझना आसान है।

आप जानते हैं कि मैं यह पुस्तक इसलिए नहीं लिख रहा हूं क्योंकि मैं लेखक या लेखक बनना चाहता हूं ऐसा इसलिए है क्योंकि मेरी नियति को इस तरह से डिजाइन किया गया है। मुझे पता है कि मेरा यह काम दुनिया में सबसे ज्यादा बिकने वाला है, लेकिन इसका कोई फायदा नहीं है क्योंकि मैं अपनी नियति जानता हूं, मैं अपने अंतिम मसौदे के छपने से पहले बाहर निकलने के लिए तैयार हूं मैं अपनी जीत का लुत्फ नहीं उठा पा रहा था। यह इस कारण से नहीं है कि मैं चिकित्सकीय रूप से बीमार हूँ या कुछ और। तथ्य यह है कि कई गुरु इसे मौखिक और शारीरिक रूप से सिखाते हैं लेकिन उनका लेखन समाप्त हो सकता है। सभी की अलग-अलग तरीकों से मौत हुई है। मैं जानता हूं कि यह मेरी नियति है और मैं इसे ज्यों का त्यों स्वीकार करूंगा।

Acknowledgements

This book will give you a base in understanding that will lead to a new base of vedic mathematics. As most of the peoples don't know the techniques derived from 16 sutras in the Vedas, which are earliest literature of ancient hindus in india. Further in this book I will let you know about the endless source of knowledge and wisdom, providing practical knowledge in all spheres of life.

This techniques used in this book are traditional along with some encapsulated with immense and brilliant mathematical knowledge of ancient Indians, who had made fundamental contributions to mathematics in the form of the decimal numerals, zero and infinity.

Acknowledgements

यह पुस्तक आपको समझने के लिए एक आधार प्रदान करेगी जो वैदिक गणित के एक नए आधार की ओर ले जाएगी। जैसा कि अधिकांश लोग वेदों में 16 सूत्रों से प्राप्त तकनीकों को नहीं जानते हैं, जो भारत में प्राचीन हिंदुओं के सबसे पुराने साहित्य हैं। आगे इस पुस्तक में मैं आपको जीवन के सभी क्षेत्रों में व्यावहारिक ज्ञान प्रदान करने वाले ज्ञान और ज्ञान के अंतहीन स्रोत के बारे में बताऊंगा।

इस पुस्तक में उपयोग की गई तकनीकें पारंपरिक हैं, साथ ही प्राचीन भारतीयों के विशाल और शानदार गणितीय ज्ञान के साथ कुछ एनकैप्सुलेटेड हैं, जिन्होंने दशमलव अंकों, शून्य और अनंत के रूप में गणित में मौलिक योगदान दिया था।

Prologue

Why the antyayordasakepi

Let me start by giving you a problem? What is 2+2 is..........some of you must be thinking that its so simple that is equal to 4......some of them must be thinking why this simple question I in this chapter going to discuss the psychology of student..

If I put forward the same question then there are many different thinkers.

Case 1: those who over think and say it can be integrated to get the sum or we should consider it with a small element and then integrate it with definite limits.

Case 2: those who does think and say it can not be solved.

Case 3: those who simple claim the answer to be 4.

This is the psychology of students and people used to overthink beyond this.

From the survey of my last 5 years I came across many people who claim that they don't have interest in mathematics, they are some who even quote that they hate mathematics. One of my friend even claim that he opted for biology because he can't carry out with mathematics any more..the traditional method of mathematics is letting the students to crease from mathematics...so I thought of writing this book on the vedic mathematics sutra "antyayordasakepi".

You know what this book is just giving you a brief of mathematical formulas in just some glist

Prologue

अंत्ययोरदासकपेी क्यों

मैं आपको एक समस्या देकर शुरू करता हूँ 2+2 क्या है.........आप में से कुछ सोच रहे होंगे कि यह इतना सरल है कि 4 के बराबर है...... उनमें से कुछ सोच रहे होंगे कि यह सरल प्रश्न में इस अध्याय में छात्र के मनोविज्ञान पर चर्चा करने जा रहा हूँ

अगर मैं एक ही सवाल सामने रखूं तो कई अलग-अलग विचारक हैं

केस 1: जो लोग सोचते हैं और कहते हैं कि इस योग प्राप्त करने के लिए एकीकृत किया जा सकता है या हमें इस एक छोटे से तत्व के रूप में मानना चाहिए और फिर इसे निश्चित सीमाओं के साथ एकीकृत करना चाहिए।

केस 2: जो सोचते हैं और कहते हैं उन्हें हल नहीं किया जा सकता है

केस 3: जो सामान्य दावा करते हैं कि उत्तर 4 है

यह छात्रों का मनोविज्ञान है और लोग इससे पर सोचते थे।

मेरे पिछले 5 वर्षों के सर्वेक्षण से मैं ऐसे कई लोगों के संपर्क में आया जो दावा करते हैं कि उन्हें गणित में कोई दिलचस्पी नहीं है, वे कुछ ऐसे भी हैं जो यह भी कहते हैं कि वे गणित से नफरत करते हैं मेरे एक मित्र का यह भी दावा है कि उसने जीव विज्ञान को चुना क्योंकि वह अब गणित के साथ नहीं चल सकता..गणित की पारंपरिक पद्धति छात्रों को गणित से आगे बढ़ने देती है...इसलिए मैंने इस पुस्तक को वैदिक गणित सूत्र पर लिखने के बारे में सोचा "अंत्ययोरदासकपेी"।

आप जानते हैं कि यह पुस्तक आपको केवल कुछ झलक में गणितीय सूत्रों का संक्षिप्त विवरण दे रही है

CHAPTER ONE

Ekadhikena purvena

The literal meaning of this sutra is *" by one more than the previous one"*.

The whole procedure can be summarized as

Step1: add the unit digits column wise

Step 2: when the running total becomes greater than 10, put a dot or tick on that number.

Step3: move ahead with the excess of ten and add it to the next digit of the column.

Step 4: lastly count the number of dots or tick and note it down to the number next to the unit place figure and add the two....

Let understand this by means of example:

1. Add 486+645+987

   a. In this sutra, 6+4=10, so take away the excess 0 and add it with the next digit 7 of the column i.e. 0+7=7. Write the final sum 7 in the remainder column. Put a bar over 4.

   b. 8+5=13, so write it excess 3 in the remainder column. Put a dot over 5. The excess will be further added to 8, making it equal to 11. Hence mark on 8 and write 1 in the answer column.

c. 4+6=10, so mark on 6 and move with the excess 0 to be added to the next number of the remainder column. Write 0+9=9 in the total column. Now count the number of bars in each column and place it down to the number next to the unit place as done. And then add to get final result

CHAPTER TWO

एकाधिकेन पूर्वेण

इस सूत्र का शाब्दिक अर्थ है "पिछले एक से एक अधिक"।

पूरी प्रक्रिया के रूप में संक्षेप किया जा सकता है

Step1: इकाई अंक कॉलम के अनुसार जोड़ें.

स्टेप 2: जब रनिंग टोटल 10 से ज़्यादा हो जाए तो उस नंबर पर डॉट या टिक लगाएं।

चरण 3: दस के आधिक्य के साथ आगे बढ़ें और इस कॉलम के अगले अंक में जोड़ दें।

चरण 4: अंत में डॉट्स की संख्या गिनें या टिक करें और इस यूनिट प्लेस फिगर के आगे की संख्या पर नोट करें और दोनों को जोड़ें...।

इस उदाहरण के माध्यम से समझते हैं:

1. 486+645+987 जोड़ें.

एक। इस सूत्र में 6+4=10 है, इसलिए अतिरिक्त 0 को हटा दें और इस कॉलम के अगले अंक 7 यानी 0+7=7 के साथ जोड़ दें अंतिम योग 7 को शेष कॉलम में लिखें 4 पर बार लगाएं।

बी। 8+5=13, अत: इस शेषफल वाले कॉलम में अतिरिक्त 3 लिखें 5 पर एक बिंदि लगाएं। अतिरिक्त को 8 में जोड़ा जाएगा, जिससे यह 11 के बराबर हो जाएगा। इसलिए 8 पर निशान लगाएं और उत्तर कॉलम में 1 लिखें।

सी। 4+6=10, इसलिए 6 पर निशान लगाएं और शेष कॉलम की अगली संख्या में जोड़े जाने के लिए अतिरिक्त 0 के साथ आगे बढ़ें। कुल कॉलम में

0+9=9 लिखो। अब प्रत्येक कॉलम में बार की संख्या की गणना करें और इसे इकाई स्थान के बगल में संख्या के रूप में नीचे रखो और फिर अंतिम परिणाम प्राप्त करने के लिए जोड़ें।

• 4 •

CHAPTER THREE

Nikhilam navatascaramam dasatah

" all from nine and last from ten"

Subtraction

This method works faster when subtraction is done from multiples of 10.

Rule:

Start moving from right to left. Replace every zero from the left with a 9 and the last zero with a 10. The extreme left digit before zero will get reduced by 1. Now do the simple subtracting without worrying about mistakes.

1. When the digit at minuend is greater than subtrahend digit, normal subtraction is done.
2. In case the upper digit is less than lower digit, we take the complement of the difference as shown:
3. This complement of the last digit is taken from 10 and the complements of the rest of the digit are taken from 9.

4. When you arrive at a stage where there is no need to take the complement, subtract 1 extra from that column.

Let us consider with an problem

1. 854-569=?

    a. Since 4<9, we take the complement of the difference of the digit. This complement will be taken from 10. The difference of 9 and 4 is 5. From the complement table it is evident that the complement of 5 is 5, so write 5 at the unit place.
    b. Again, 5<6, so we take the complement of the difference of two digit, but this time the complement is taken from 9 instead of 10. As the sutra suggest all from 9 and last from 10. The difference of 6-5=1 and its complement from 9 is 9-1=8 so write 8 at the ten's place.
    c. The difference of the digit at the hundred's place can easily be carried out as 8>5. So we don't need to take the complement for the third column. As we are now out of the complement, subtract 1 more in this column. Hence, instead of subtracting 8-5, we subtract 8-5-1=2.....285

Multiplication

This sutra works better when both the multiplicand and multiplier are very close to the base. The base should be in the form of 10^n, where n is a natural number.

Rule:

1. Write the two numbers to be multiplied above and below at the right side of your notebook.

2. Write the deviation of multiplicand and multiplier from the base and place them next to the digit to be multiplied.
3. The final result will have twoparts.

   a. The left hand part will obtained by cross operation of two numbers written diagonally.
   b. The right side of the answer will be obtained by multiplying the deviations.

4. The number of digits in the right hand part will be in accordance to the number of zeros in the base number. In simple words, if the base is 100, the right hand part will have two digits and if the base is 1000, the right hand part will have three digits.
5. In case there is lesser number of digits in the right side, accommodate as many zeros before the right hand part so that the total number of digits in that part is equal to the number of zeros in the base.
6. Here is the table that will guide you in deciding the number of digits to be placed on the right hand side.

Case 1: when both number are below the base

1. Multiply 95 by 91

   a. Both the numbers are closer to the base 100, so take base=100. Deviation of 95= 95-100=-5, deviation of 91=91-100=-9
   b. Put the deviation at the right side along with the number to be multiplied.
   c. Write the left hand digit by cross operation of any of the two diagonals. Here 95-9=86 or 91-5=86 is

written in the left hand part.

d. The right hand digit will be the multiplication of the deviation.

Case 2: when both the number are above the base

1. Multiply 105 by 104?

    a. Both the numbers are closer to the base 100, so take base=100. Deviation of 105=105-100=+5, deviation of 104=104-100=+4

    b. Put the deviation at the right side along with the number to be multiplied.

    c. Write the left hand digit by cross operation of any of the two diagonals.

    d. The right hand digit will be the multiplication of the deviation

Case 3: when one number is above the base and another is less than the base.

1. Mutliply 122 by 98?

    a. Both the numbers are closer to the base 100, so take base=100, deviation of 122=122-100=+22, deviation of 98=98-100=-2

    b. Put the deviation at the right side along with the number to be multiplied.

    c. Write the left hand digit by cross operation of any of the two diagonals.

    d. The right hand digit will be the multiplication of the deviation.

e. When there is a minus sign at the right hand product, use the nilhilam formulae which states, " all from 9 and last term from 100." Hence subtract the right hand digit (-44) from 100 and left hand part 120 will get diminished by 1, i.e 120-1=119

Case 4: adjustment of right side digit of the product.

CHAPTER FOUR

नखिलिं नवतश्चरामं दसतः

"सभी नौ से और अंतिम दस से"

घटाव

यह विधि तेजी से काम करती है जब 10 के गुणकों से घटाव किया जाता है।

नियम:

दाएं से बाएं घूमना शुरू करें बाईं ओर के प्रत्येक शून्य को 9 से और अंतिम शून्य को 10 से बदल दें शून्य से पहले के अंतिम बाएं अंक को 1 से कम कर दिया जाएगा। अब गलतियों की चिंता किए बिना सरल घटाव करें।

1. जब माइन्यूएंड का अंक घटाए गए अंक से बड़ा होता है, तो सामान्य घटाव किया जाता है।

2. यदि ऊपरी अंक नीचिले अंक से कम है, तो हम दिखाए गए अनुसार अंतर का पूरक लेते हैं:

3. अंतिम अंक का यह पूरक 10 से लिया जाता है और शेष अंक का पूरक 9 से लिया जाता है।

4. जब आप एक ऐसी स्थिति में पहुंचें जहां पूरक लेने की कोई आवश्यकता नहीं है, तो उस कॉलम से 1 अतिरिक्त घटाएं।

आइए एक समस्या पर विचार करें

1. 854-569=?

एक। चूंकि 4<9, हम अंक के अंतर का पूरक लेते हैं यह पूरक 10 से लिया जाएगा। 9 और 4 का अंतर 5 है। पूरक तालिका से स्पष्ट है कि 5 का पूरक

5 है, इसलिए इकाई के स्थान पर 5 लिखिे

बी। दोबारा, 5<6, इसलिए हम दो अंको के अंतर का पूरक लेते हैं, लेकिन इस बार पूरक 10 के बजाय 9 से लिया गया है जैसा कि सूत्र 9 से सभी और 10 से अंतिम का सुझाव देता है 6-5 का अंतर = 1 और 9 से इसका पूरक 9-1=8 है तो दहाई के स्थान पर 8 लिखिे

सी। सौ के स्थान पर अंक का अंतर आसानी से 8>5 के रूप में किया जा सकता है इसलिए हमें तीसरे कॉलम के लिए कॉम्प्लिमेंट लेने की जरूरत नहीं है जैसा कि अब हम पूरक से बाहर हैं, इस कॉलम में 1 और घटाएं इसलिए, 8-5 घटाने के बजाय, हम 8-5-1=2.....285 घटाते हैं

गुणा

यह सूत्र तब बेहतर काम करता है जब गुण्य और गुणक दोनों आधार के बहुत करीब हों। आधार 10n के रूप में होना चाहिए, जहाँ n एक प्राकृत संख्या है

नियम:

1. गुणा की जाने वाली दो संख्याएं ऊपर और नीचे अपनी कॉपी के दाहिनी ओर लिखिे

2. आधार से गुण्य और गुणक का विचलन लिखिए और उन्हें गुणा किए जाने वाले अंक के आगे रखिए।

3. अंतिम परिणाम के दो भाग होंगे।

एक। बाएं हाथ का हिस्सा तिरछे लिखे दो नंबरों के क्रॉस ऑपरेशन से प्राप्त होगा।

बी। विचलनों को गुणा करने पर दाहिनी ओर का उत्तर प्राप्त होगा।

4. दाहिने हाथ के भाग में अंकों की संख्या आधार संख्या में शून्य की संख्या के अनुसार होगी। सरल शब्दों में यदि आधार 100 है तो दाहिने भाग में दो अंक होंगे और यदि आधार 1000 है तो दाहिने भाग में तीन अंक होंगे

5. यदि दाहिने भाग में अंकों की संख्या कम है, तो दाहिने भाग के पहले जितने शून्य हों, उतने शून्य लगा दें कि उस भाग के अंकों की संख्या आधार के शून्यों की संख्या के बराबर हो जाए।

6. यहां वह तालिका दी गई है जो दाहिनी ओर रखे जाने वाले अंकों की संख्या तय करने में आपका मार्गदर्शन करेगी।

केस 1: जब दोनों नंबर बेस के नीचे हों

1. 95 को 91 से गुणा करें

एक। दोनों संख्याएं आधार 100 के करीब हैं, इसलिए आधार = 100 लों 95 का विचलन= 95-100=-5, 91 का विचलन=91-100=-9

बी। गुणा की जाने वाली संख्या के साथ विचलन को दाईं ओर रखों

सी। दोनों विकिरणों में से किसी एक की अनुप्रस्थ संक्रिया द्वारा बाएं हाथ का अंक लिखिए। यहां बाएं हाथ के हिस्से में 95-9=86 या 91-5=86 लिखा है।

डी। दाहिनि हाथ का अंक विचलन का गुणा होगा।

स्थिति 2: जब दोनों संख्याएं आधार से ऊपर हों

1. 105 को 104 से गुणा करें?

एक। दोनों संख्याएं आधार 100 के करीब हैं, इसलिए आधार = 100 लों 105 का विचलन=105-100=+5, 104 का विचलन=104-100=+4

बी। गुणा की जाने वाली संख्या के साथ विचलन को दाईं ओर रखों

सी। दोनों विकिरणों में से किसी एक की अनुप्रस्थ संक्रिया द्वारा बाएं हाथ का अंक लिखिए।

डी। दाहिनि हाथ का अंक विचलन का गुणा होगा

स्थिति 3: जब एक संख्या आधार से ऊपर हो और दूसरी संख्या आधार से छोटी हो।

1. 122 को 98 से गुणा करें?

एक। दोनों संख्याएं आधार 100 के करीब हैं, इसलिए आधार = 100 लें, 122 का विचलन=122-100=+22, 98 का विचलन=98-100=-2

बी। गुणा की जाने वाली संख्या के साथ विचलन को दाईं ओर रखों

सी। दोनों विकिरणों में से किसी एक की अनुप्रस्थ संक्रिया द्वारा बाएं हाथ का अंक लिखिए।

डी। दाहिनि हाथ का अंक विचलन का गुणा होगा।

इ। जब उत्पाद के दाहिने हाथ पर एक ऋण चिह्न होता है, तो निहिलम सूत्र का उपयोग करें, जो कहता है, "9 से सभी और 100 से अंतिम पद।" इसलिए 100 में से दाहिने हाथ का अंक (-44) घटाएं और बाएं हाथ का भाग 120 1 से कम हो जाएगा, यानी 120-1=119

स्थिति 4: गणनफल के दाईं ओर के अंक का समायोजन।

CHAPTER FIVE

Urdhva tiryagbhyam

" vertically and crosswise"

This sutra is applicable to multiplication of algebraic equations. The present chapter will deal with the following types of equation:

- Binomials
- Polynomial with equal number of terms
- Polynomial with unequal number of terms

The meaning and its working has been explicity.

Step 1: first, write the two variables on the top and put the coefficients from each equation below. Apply the urdhya tiryagbhyam vedic sutra. Remember, the carry-over to the preceding column as done in multiplication will not be executed here

Vertical |sum of cross wise| vertical

Step2: starting from the right, add the variables to these coefficient in the following manner.

The vertical multiplication of y X y is 8. So add y^2 to 8 as this is the coefficient of y^2.

The cross wise multiplication of x and y, yields result 10, add xy to 10.

The vertical multiplication of x and x yields 3 as a result so this is the coefficient of x^2.

Considering some problems:

1. Multiply $(8x-3y)$ by $(2x+4y)$

    a. Write the two variables on top and their coefficients along their respective signs below them.
    b. Do vertical and crosswise multiplication from the right. The multiplication will have the following steps-

        i. $4 \times (-3)=(-12)$------- this is the given vertical product
        ii. $8 \times 4 + 2 \times (-3) = 32 - 6 = 26$-------- the sum of cross wise multiplication)
        iii. $8 \times 2 = 16$---------- the product of vertical extreme left

    c. Place the respective variables with their coefficient, i.e. place y^2 to -12, xy to 26 and x^2 to 16......hence the result is $16x^2+26xy-16y^2$.

2. multiply 3x-7y by 2x-5y

    a. write down the variable on the top and their respective coefficient below , with the proper sign.
    b. Do vertical and cross wise multiplication from the right and place the proper variables to the coefficients
    c. The product will be $6x^2 -29xy+35y^2$.

3. Further can be understand by 1234321 pattern.

CHAPTER SIX

ऊर्ध्व तर्ियग्भ्यम्

"ऊर्ध्वाधर और आड्-तिर्छे"

यह सूत्र बीजगणितीय समीकरणों के गुणन पर लागू होता है। वर्तमान अध्याय निम्नलिखित प्रकार के समीकरणों से निपटेगा:

? द्विपद

? समान पदों वाली बहुपद

? असमान पदों की संख्या वाला बहुपद

अर्थ और उसका कार्य स्पष्ट किया गया है।

चरण 1: सबसे पहले, शीर्ष पर दो चर लिखें और प्रत्येक समीकरण से गुणांक नीचे रखों। उर्ध्व तर्ियग्भ्य वैदिक सूत्र का प्रयोग करों। याद रखें, पूर्ववर्ती कॉलम में ले जाने के लिए जैसा कि गुणा में किया गया है, यहां निष्पादित नहीं किया जाएगा।

लंबवत |क्रॉस बार का योग| खड़ा

Step2: दाईं ओर से शुरू करते हुए, चरों को इन गुणांकों में निम्नलिखित तरीके से जोड़ें।

y X y का ऊर्ध्वाधर गुणा 8 है इसलिए y2 को 8 में जोड़ें क्योंकि यह y2 का गुणांक है।

x और y का आड्-तिर्छे गुणा करने पर परिणाम 10 मिलता है, xy को 10 में जोड़ दें।

x और x का लंबवत गुणन परिणाम के रूप में 3 देता है इसलिए यह x2 का गुणांक है।

कुछ समस्याओं को ध्यान में रखते हुए:

1. (8x-3y) को (2x+4y) से गुणा करें

एक। शीर्ष पर दो चर और उनके नीचे उनके संबंधित चिह्नों के साथ उनके गुणांक लिखें।

बी। दाईं ओर से वर्टिकल और क्रॉसवाइज गुणा करो। गुणन के निम्नलिखित चरण होंगे-

मौ। 4 x (-3)=(-12)------- यह दिया गया लंबवत गुणनफल है।

द्वितीय। 8 x 4 + 2 x (-3) = 32 − 6 = 26-------- क्रॉस वार गुणन का योग)

तृतीय। 8 x 2 = 16 ---------- लंबवत चरम बाएं का उत्पाद

सी। संबंधित चरों को उनके गुणांक के साथ रखें, यानी y2 को -12, xy को 26 और x2 को 16 में रखें... इसलिए परिणाम 16x2+26xy-16y2 है।

2. 3x-7y को 2x-5y से गुणा करें

एक। शीर्ष पर चर और उनके संबंधित गुणांक को उचित चिह्न के साथ नीचे लिखें।

बी। दाईं ओर से वर्टिकल और क्रॉस वाइज गुणा करें और उचित चरों को गुणांकों में रखें।

सी। गुणनफल 6x2 -29xy+35y2 होगा।

3. आगे 1234321 पैटर्न से समझा जा सकता है।

CHAPTER SEVEN

Paravartya yojayet

"transpose and apply"

The well known rule relating to transposition enjoins an invariable change of sign with every change in side.

This method is applicable for all sorts of linear simultaneous equation. The cross multiplication method taught in respective classes during current curriculum is somewhat derived from this sutra... this sutra is cyclic in nature hence is it can be used both in multiplication and division as well.

For x, we start with the y- coefficient and the independent term and cross multiply them in the forward direction. The sign between the two cross multiplication is minus. For y, we the start with the independent term and x coefficient and cross multiply them in backward direction. The sign between the cross multiplication result is minus.

Let us consider two equation of the form:

$a_1x + b_{1y}=c_1$----------(1)

$a_2x + b_2y=c_2$-----------(2)

in order to get the numerator of x, we leave the coefficients of x and write the coefficient of y and the independent term and cross multiply them with a minus sign in between the cross product in the rightward direction is given as $= b_1c_2-b_2c_1$

again, to get the numerator of y, we leave the coefficient of y and take only the coefficient of x and the independent term into consideration. As you know, the sutra moves in a cyclic order, so we have to start with the independent term first. Cross multiplication of the independent term and coefficient of x will give the numerator of y....$=c_1a_2-a_1c_2$

the denominator of both the variables x and y will remain same. The cross product of the coefficient of the variable in the backward direction gives us the result= $a_1b_2-a_2b_1$.

.....i will suggest you must go through this question in order to get the solution...

1. Solve of x and y: 2x+3y=7; 3x+7y=13.
2. Solve of x and y:5x+3y=12; 6x+2y=45.

CHAPTER EIGHT

परवर्त्य योजायेत्

"स्थानांतरति करें और लागू करें"

स्थानान्तरण से संबंधति सुप्रसिद्ध नियम पक्ष में प्रत्येक परविर्तन के साथ चन्हि के एक अपरविर्तनीय परविर्तन को जोड़ता है।

यह वधि सभी प्रकार के रैखिक युगपत समीकरणों के लिए लागू होती है। वर्तमान पाठ्यक्रम के दौरान संबंधति कक्षाओं में सखिाई जाने वाली क्रॉस गणन वधि कुछ हद तक इस सूत्र से ली गई है ... यह सूत्र प्रकृति में चक्रीय है इसलिए इसका उपयोग गुणा और भाग दोनों में भी कयिा जा सकता है।

x के लिए, हम y- गुणांक और स्वतंत्र पद से शरू करते हैं और उन्हें आगे की दशिा में गुणा करते हैं। दो क्रॉस गणन के बीच का चन्हि माइनस है। Y के लिए, हम स्वतंत्र शब्द और x गुणांक से शरू करते हैं और उन्हें पीछे की दशिा में गुणा करते हैं। क्रॉस गणन परणिाम के बीच का चन्हि माइनस है।

आइए फॉर्म के दो समीकरणों पर वचिार करें:

$a_1x + b_1y = c_1$ ----------(1)

$a_2x + b_2y = c_2$ -----------(2)

x का अंश प्राप्त करने के लिए, हम x के गुणांक को छोड़ देते हैं और y का गुणांक और स्वतंत्र शब्द लखिते हैं और क्रॉस गणनफल के बीच में क्रॉस गणनफल के बीच उन्हें दाईं ओर की दशिा में गुणा करते हैं, जो इस प्रकार दयिा जाता है = $b_1c_2 \neg -b_2c_1$

फिर से, y का अंश प्राप्त करने के लिए, हम y के गुणांक को छोड़ देते हैं और केवल x के गुणांक और स्वतंत्र पद को ध्यान में रखते हैं। जैसा कि आप जानते हैं, सूत्र एक चक्रीय क्रम में चलता है, इसलिए हमें पहले स्वतंत्र पद से प्रारंभ करना होगा। स्वतंत्र पद का क्रॉस गुणन और x का गुणांक $y....=c1a2-a1c2$ का अंश देगा

दोनों चरों x और y का हर समान रहेगा। पिछली दिशा में चर के गुणांक का क्रॉस उत्पाद हमें परिणाम $= a1b2-a2b1$ देता है

..... मैं सुझाव दूंगा कि समाधान प्राप्त करने के लिए आपको इस प्रश्न को अवश्य पढ़ना चाहिए...

1. x और y को हल करें: $2x+3y=7$; $3x+7y=13$.
2. x और y को हल करें: $5x+3y=12$; $6x+2y=45$.

CHAPTER NINE

Anurupye sunyamanyat

" if one is in ratio, other one is zero."

This is a special type of simultaneous equation, which at the very first instance looks very hard due to the involvement of large numbers, but the vedic method makes it simple. The vedic sutra says- if one is in ratio, the other one is zero. In the simple language, whenever the ratio of x or y is equal to that of the independent term, put the ratio of y or x=0

Let take a problem and then solve it:

1. Solve for x and y : 5x+8y=40; and 10x+11y=80

    a. The ratio of the coefficient of x is 1:2 and the ratio of the independent term is also 1:2. The vedic sutra in this special case says- if one is in the ratio, the other one is zero.
    b. Since the ratio of x is equal to the ratio of the independent term, y=0. Put y=0 in either of the equation to get the value of x
    c. For y=0, 10x= 80 hence x=8
    d. The solution thus gives x=8 or y=0 is the solution.

CHAPTER TEN

अनुरूप्य सून्यमान्यात

"यदि एक अनुपात में हैं, तो दूसरा शून्य है"

यह एक विशिष्ट प्रकार का युगपत समीकरण है, जो पहली बार में बडी़ संख्याओं के शामिल होने के कारण बहुत कठिन लगता है, लेकिन वैदिक विधि इसे सरल बनाती है। वैदिक सूत्र कहता है- यदि एक अनुपात में हैं, तो दूसरा शून्य है। सरल भाषा में, जब भी x या y का अनुपात स्वतंत्र पद के अनुपात के बराबर हो, तो y या x=0 का अनुपात रखें।

एक समस्या लें और फिर उसे हल करें:

1. x और y के लिए हल करें: 5x+8y=40; और 10x+11y=80

एका। x के गुणांक का अनुपात 1:2 है और स्वतंत्र पद का अनुपात भी 1:2 है। इस विशिष्ट मामले में वैदिक सूत्र कहता है- यदि एक अनुपात में हैं, तो दूसरा शून्य है।

बी। चूँकि x का अनुपात स्वतंत्र पद के अनुपात के बराबर है, y=0. x का मान प्राप्त करने के लिए किसी भी समीकरण में y=0 रखें।

सी। y=0 के लिए, 10x= 80 इसलिए x=8

डी। समाधान इस प्रकार देता है x=8 या y=0 समाधान है।

CHAPTER ELEVEN

Sankalana-vyavakalanabhyam

(by addition and subtraction)

As said earlier, this sutra simply means- addition and subtraction. Whenever the coefficient of x in the 1st equation is equal to the coefficient of y in the 2nd equation and vice-versa, this sutra works better.

Let us take an example and see its modus operandi.

1. Solve for x and y: 23x+31y=18; 31x+23y=90

    a. As the coefficient of x in first equation is equal to the coefficient of y in second equation i.e. 23
    b. As the coefficient of y in first equation is equal to the coefficient of x in second equation i.e. 31
    c. To apply with this sutra, add both the sutras and subtract on eithernotes. You get the solution x=1/2 and y=-7/2.

CHAPTER TWELVE

संकलन-

वयावकलानाभ्यम

"जोड़ और घटाव द्वारा"

जैसा कि पहले कहा गया है, इस सूत्र का सीधा सा अर्थ है- जोड़ और घटाव। जब भी पहले समीकरण में x का गुणांक दूसरे समीकरण में y के गुणांक के बराबर होता है और इसके विपिरीत, यह सूत्र बेहतर काम करता है।

आइए एक उदाहरण लेते हैं और इसकी कार्यप्रणाली देखते हैं।

1. x और y के लिए हल करें: 23x+31y=18; 31x+23y=90

एक। क्योंकि पहले समीकरण में x का गुणांक दूसरे समीकरण में y के गुणांक के बराबर है, अर्थात 23

बी। क्योंकि पहले समीकरण में y का गुणांक दूसरे समीकरण में x के गुणांक के बराबर है यानी 31

सी। इस सूत्र के साथ प्रयोग करने के लिए, दोनों सूत्रों को जोड़ें और किसी भी नोट पर घटाएं। आपको समाधान x=1/2 और y=-7/2 मिलता है।

CHAPTER THIRTEEN

Puranapuranabhyam

" by completion and non-completion"

Completion of the base number in the multiple of 10. This sutra helps you to form a group of two or more numbers in such a way that their unit digits add up to the multiple of 10.

This method is useful for large calculations. The vedic sutra is based on completion or non- completion of a base number that is the multiple of 10. The calculation(large calculation in particular) is made easier by pairing numbers which complete a base(i.e. in multiple of 10). The pairing becomes easier if you remember the complement of the digits. Here is a list of pairs that complement each other.

Rule:

1. Spot those number which if paired would result in a rounded result. The above complement table will help you in making such pair immediately.

2. Rearrange the numbers and add as per the pairing of numbers..

Let take a summation

1. Add: 26+59+394+66+11+14

a. Here, the complete observation shows us that 26+14 are likely to yield a rounded result. The same would be the case if 59 and 11 were paired. Moreover, the pair 394 and 66 yield a rounded result.
b. Rearrange the pair and add as per the pairing done above.

26+14+59+11+394+66

40+70+460

40+460+70

500+70

570

CHAPTER FOURTEEN

पूरणपूराणभ्यं

"पूरा होने और पूरा न होने से"

10 के गुणक में आधार संख्या का पूरा होना। यह सूत्र आपको दो या दो से अधिक संख्याओं का एक समूह बनाने में इस तरह से मदद करता है कि उनके इकाई अंक 10 के गुणक में जुड़ते हैं

यह विधि बड़ी गणनाओं के लिए उपयोगी है वैदिक सूत्र एक आधार संख्या के पूरा होने या न पूरा होने पर आधारित है जो 10 का गुणक है गणना (विशिष रूप से बड़ी गणना) को उन संख्याओं की जोड़ी बनाकर आसान बनाया जाता है जो एक आधार को पूरा करती है (अर्थात 10 के गुणक में)। यदि आप अंकों के पूरक को याद रखते हैं तो जोड़ी बनाना आसान हो जाता है यहां उन जोड़ियों की सूची दी गई है जो एक दूसरे के पूरक हैं

नियम:

1. उन संख्याओं को चिन्हित करें जिन्हें जोड़ने पर परिणाम गोल होगा। उपरोक्त पूरक तालिका आपको ऐसी जोड़ी तुरंत बनाने में मदद करेगी।

2. संख्याओं को पुनर्व्यवस्थित करें और संख्याओं की जोड़ी के अनुसार जोड़ें

आइए एक योग लें

1. जोड़ें: 26+59+394+66+11+14

एक। यहाँ, पूर्ण अवलोकन हमें दिखाता है कि 26+14 के एक गोल परिणाम प्राप्त करने की संभावना है यदि 59 और 11 को जोड़ा जाता तो

भी ऐसा ही होता। इसके अलावा, 394 और 66 की जोड़ी एक गोल परिणाम देती है।

बी। जोड़ी को पुनर्व्यवस्थित करें और ऊपर की जोड़ी के अनुसार जोड़ें।

26+14+59+11+394+66

40+70+460

40+460+70

500+70

570

CHAPTER FIFTEEN

Yavadunam

" the deficiency"

Yavadunam tavaduni kritya varganea yojayet

This vedic sub-sutra is used for squaring number which are closer to the base(10^n). with a little practice, though, you can extent to numbers which are further form the base using the sub-base, provided the sub- base is a multiple of 10^n.

The vedic sutra simply says

Find the extent or deficiency of a number to be a squared with respect to its base. This extent or deficiency is termed here as deviation.

Set up the square of the deviation at the end.

The sutra works better when the number to squared is near the base number like 10, 100, 1000, ... or is the multiple of the base number like 20, 30, 40,.....

Lets us understand it in two parts

Part 1:

When the number is near the base number.

This can be solved as

LHS: number + deviation

RHS: square of deviation

The RHS will contain the same number of digits as the number of zero in the base. The excess digit, if any, will be carried over to LHS and the deficit digit, if any, will be filled up by putting the zero to left of RHS.

Part 2

When the base is not in the form of 10^n but the multiple of 10.

The answer will be arrived at in two parts

The RHS part of the answer will be the square of deviation from the base. The LHS part of the answer should be written with utmost care, LHS=(number to be squared+deviation)X sub-base.

Let us take a problem:

1. Find the square of 13?

    a. Here deviation from the base is 13-10=3
    b. So the square will be $13+3/(3)^2$
    c. This gives the LHS to be 16 and RHS to be 9....so the answer will be 169.

2. Find the square of 97?

    a. Here deviation from the base is 97-100=-3
    b. So the square will be $97-3/(-3)^2$
    c. This gives the LHS to be 94 and RHS to be 9 written as 09 because the base has two zero so RHS has same number of digit....so the answer will be 9409.

3. Find the square of 47?

    a. Here deviation from the sub-base is 47-5=-3
    b. So the square will be $(47-3)X5/(-3)^2$
    c. This gives the LHS to be 220 and RHS to be 9....so the answer will be 2209.

Yavadunam

The formula works better when the number to cubed is near base. The base should be in the form of 10^n, where n is a natural number. This formula has limited application.

Working rule:

1. Check whether the number is near the base 10,100,1000,... or not.
2. Find the excess or deficit number from the base.
3. The whole operation is to be performed in three parts. In the 1st part, add twice the excess/deficit to the original number.
4. 2nd part=new excess(number obtained in 1st part-base)X original excess/deficit.
5. 3rd part=cube of excess.

Mathemactically, if a= original number and d=deviation(excess/deficit from the base) then the whole operation can be summed up as-

$$a^3=a+2d/[(a+2d)-base]Xd/d^3$$

let take a problem:

1. Find the cube of 12?

a. a=12 is near to the base 10 hence deviation is +2
b. part 1 is a+2d= 12+2x2=12+4=16
c. part 2 is (16-10)x2=12
d. part 3 is $(2)^3=8$
e. combining all as 16|12|8........17|2|8......=1728 is the answer

CHAPTER SIXTEEN

यवदूनम

"कमी"

यवदूनाम तवदूनिकृत्य वर्गानं योजायेत्

इस वैदिक उप-सूत्र का उपयोग वर्ग संख्या के लिए किया जाता है जो आधार (10n) के करीब हो। थोड़े अभ्यास के साथ, हालांकि, आप उन संख्याओं तक विस्तार कर सकते हैं जो आगे उप-आधार का उपयोग करके आधार बनाते हैं, बशर्ते कि उप-आधार 10n का गुणज हो।

वैदिक सूत्र बस कहता है

आधार के संबंध में किसी संख्या का वर्ग होने की सीमा या कमी का पता लगाएं। इस सीमा या कमी को यहाँ वचिलन कहा जाता है।

अंत में वचिलन का वर्ग सेट करो

सूत्र बेहतर काम करता है जब वर्ग की संख्या 10, 100, 1000, ... जैसे आधार संख्या के पास हो या 20, 30, 40, ... जैसे आधार संख्या का गुणक हो।

आइए इसे दो भागों में समझते हैं

भाग 1:

जब नंबर आधार नंबर के पास हो।

इसे इस प्रकार हल किया जा सकता है

एलएचएस: संख्या + वचिलन

RHS: वचिलन का वर्ग

RHS में उतने ही अंक होंगे जितने आधार में शून्य हौं अधिकिय अंक, यदि कोई हो, को बाएँ पक्ष में ले जाया जाएगा और कमी वाला अंक, यदि कोई हो, को दाएँ पक्ष के बाईं ओर शून्य लगाकर भरा जाएगा।

भाग 2

जब आधार 10n के रूप में नहीं बल्कि 10 के गुणक के रूप में हो।

इसका उत्तर दो भागों में मिलेगा

उत्तर का RHS भाग आधार से विचलन का वर्ग होगा। उत्तर के बाएँ भाग को अत्यंत सावधानी से लिखा जाना चाहिए, LHS = (चुकता किया जाने वाला अंक + विचलन) X उप-आधार।

आइए एक समस्या लेते हैं:

1. 13 का वर्ग ज्ञात करें?

एक। यहाँ आधार से विचलन 13-10=3 है

बी। तो वर्ग 13+3/(3)2 होगा

सी। यह LHS को 16 और RHS को 9... देता है, इसलिए उत्तर 169 होगा।

2. 97 का वर्ग ज्ञात करें?

एक। यहाँ आधार से विचलन 97-100=-3 है

बी। तो वर्ग 97-3/(-3)2 होगा

सी। यह LHS को 94 और RHS को 9 को 09 के रूप में लिखिता है क्योंकि आधार में दो शून्य होते हैं इसलिए RHS में अंकों की संख्या समान होती है... इसलिए उत्तर 9409 होगा।

3. 47 का वर्ग ज्ञात करें?

एक। यहाँ उप-आधार से विचलन 47-5=-3 है

बी। तो वर्ग (47-3)X5/(-3)2 होगा

सी। यह LHS को 220 और RHS को 9... देता है, इसलिए उत्तर 2209 होगा।

यवदुनम

सूत्र बेहतर काम करता है जब घन की संख्या आधार के पास हो। आधार 10n के रूप में होना चाहिए, जहाँ n एक प्राकृत संख्या हो। इस सूत्र

का सीमित अनुप्रयोग है।

कार्य नियम:

1. जांचें कि संख्या आधार 10,100,1000,... के पास है या नहीं।

2. आधार से आधिक्य या घाटा संख्या ज्ञात कीजिए।

3. पूरा ऑपरेशन तीन भागों में किया जाना है। पहले भाग में, मूल संख्या में दो गुना अधिक/घाटा जोड़ें।

4. दूसरा भाग=नई अधिकता (पहले भाग-आधार में प्राप्त संख्या)X मूल अधिकता/घाटा।

5. तीसरा भाग=अधिकता का घन।

गणितीय रूप से, यदि a = मूल संख्या और d = विचलन (आधार से अधिक/घाटा) तो पूरे ऑपरेशन को इस प्रकार अभिव्यक्त किया जा सकता है-

$a3=a+2d/[(a+2d)-$आधार$]Xd/d3$

चलो एक समस्या लेते हैं:

1. 12 का घन ज्ञात करें?

एक। $a=12$ आधार 10 के निकट है इसलिए विचलन +2 है।

बी। भाग 1 है $a+2d= 12+2x2=12+4=16$

सी। भाग 2 $(16-10)x2=12$ है।

डी। भाग 3 $(2)3=8$ है।

इ। सभी को मिलाकर 16|12|8........17|2|8......=1728 उत्तर है।

CHAPTER SEVENTEEN

Sunyam samyasamuccaye

"the summantion is equal to zero"

This sutra is applicable to a large number of different cases. It literally means- when the samuchchaya is the same, equal it to zero. Samuchchaya is a technical term which has several meanings under different contexts; and we shall explain them, one at a time.

Look at the following examples:

$2x+2+3x+3=4x+4+1x+1$

Minute observation proves the above equation to be a kind of quadratic equation, so it will certainly have two roots. The above type of equation can be solved by using two vedic sutras.

Now let us inspect using sunyam anyat vedic sutra which was earlier used used in solving a special type of simultaneous equation.

The formula says- if one is in ratio, the other one is zero.

Since the ratios of the constant term in both sides are equal, by sunyam anyat sutra x=0.

Now what about the second root?

The second root will be extracted by using another vedic sutra called sunyam sam samucchaye. The sutra says- if sum of numerator on both the sides are the same, equate the sum of the denominator equal to zero.

$$N_1+N_2 \text{ in LHS IS } 2+3=5$$
$$N_1+N_2 \text{ in RHS IS } 4+1=5$$

Since they are equal, we have to equate the sum of the denominator equal to zero

$$D_1+D_2=0$$
$$X+2+X+3=0 \text{ it implies } x=-5/2$$

Hence the roots are given by x=0 and x=-5/2

CHAPTER EIGHTEEN

सनुय संयममनुच्चय

"योग शून्य के बराबर है"

यह सूत्र बड़ी संख्या में विभिन्न मामलों पर लागू होता है। इसका शाब्दिक अर्थ है- जब समुच्चय एक ही हो तो उसे शून्य के बराबर कर दें। समुच्चय एक तकनीकी शब्द है जिसके विभिन्न संदर्भों में कई अर्थ हैं; और हम उन्हें एक-एक करके समझाएंगे।

निम्नलिखित उदाहरण देखें:

$$2/(x+2)+3/(x+3)=4/(x+4)+1/(x+1)$$

सूक्ष्म निरीक्षण उपरोक्त समीकरण को एक प्रकार का द्विघात समीकरण सिद्ध करता है, अत: इसके दो मूल अवश्य होंगे। उपरोक्त प्रकार के समीकरणों को दो वैदिक सूत्रों का उपयोग करके हल किया जा सकता है।

अब हम सूर्यम अन्यत वैदिक सूत्र का उपयोग करके निरीक्षण करते हैं जो पहले एक विशिष्ट प्रकार के समकालिक समीकरण को हल करने में उपयोग किया जाता था।

सूत्र कहता है- यदि एक अनुपात में हैं, तो दूसरा शून्य है।

चूंकि दोनों पक्षों में निरंतर अवधि के अनुपात बराबर हैं, सूर्यम अन्यत् सूत्र x = 0 द्वारा।

अब दूसरी जड़ के बारे में क्या?

दूसरी जड़ एक अन्य वैदिक सूत्र का उपयोग करके निकाली जाएगी जिसे सूर्य सं समुच्चय कहा जाता है। सूत्र कहता है- यदि दोनों पक्षों के

अंशों का योग समान हो तो हर के योग को शून्य के बराबर करो

LHS में N1+N2 IS 2+3=5 है

RHS में N1+N2 IS 4+1=5 है

चूँकि वे बराबर हैं, हमें हर के योग को शून्य के बराबर करना होगा

डी1+डी2=0

X+2+X+3=0 इसका मतलब x=-5/2 है

इसलिए मूल x=0 और x=-5/2 द्वारा दिए गए हैं

Our Real Identity: The Science of the Soul

This chapter has some of the most valuable information one can ever read in regard to spiritual knowledge. Within the next few pages we will establish, by Vedic evidence, the real identity and nature of the living being. Only by understanding who we are will be able to know what to do with ourselves, where we fit in this world, and so on. We will also be able to see through the bodily differences between us, and, if everyone could understand this knowledge, we could establish peace in the world. But without comprehending this information, there is little hope that true peace ever be found. Furthermore, regardless of what philosophy or religion towards which you are inclined, without understanding the detailed information about the soul, whatever spiritual progress you think you have made is, practically speaking, only superficial and hardly scratches the surface of spiritual reality. Therefore, we encourage everyone to follow the course of this chapter to enter into another level of spiritual realization.

FINDING OURSELVES

People in every part of the world are very much same in the respect that everyone is trying to find themselves. The only difference is how they do it. In this regard, everyone is a philosopher to some degree because everyone is trying to figure out how to arrange life in order to find happiness, peace of mind, and so on. But what most people assume you are talking about when you mention the idea of finding yourself is choosing the one thing you would most like to do in life. Actually, this is merely analyzing the mind and trying to discern your likes and dislikes.

Someone might want to become a businessman and work in an office in a skyscraper from nine to five everyday. Someone else may want to become a famous movie star. Another may want to become a politician, or a priest, or just learn a trade and raise a family in the countryside somewhere. There are so many things a person could do, depending on his or her ideals.

In identifying with these ideals, inclinations, or propensities, there may be certain clubs we join, or particular people with whom we associate, or activities we do with others. For example, when fans of a certain sports club, like in football or baseball, go to watch their favorite team play, they might wear the same colors as the team's uniforms. Or they may wear something like a hat or shirt with an emblem on it which signifies their loyalty to the team. They cheer for the team, maybe even fight for them and if the team wins they feel happy and proud and will celebrate with other fans.

Younger people especially may put a lot of energy into identifying with particular ideals and in expressing them in personal ways. They may wear certain clothes and hairstyles, listen to a special kind of music, and meet similarly interested friends at clubs that cater to their likes.

They may even engage in propagandizing their ideals to others. This is all part of the endeavor of trying to find our material identity.

If, however, we cannot find our own identity then we may stylize ourselves in the fashion of a particular celebrity we admire. We may dress like they do, talk like they do, way like they do, etc. But as we grow older, we may change the way we do things. We may not dress as outlandishly as we used to, or keep our hair as long, or stay out as late. So who are we? Which of these identities is the real us? As ideals are changeable, so are our names. We may call ourselves by certain names, either out of necessity, such as family name, or for individuality, like names some entertainers use. We may call ourselves Robert or Roberta, Stephen or Stephanie, Henry or Henrietta. Or we might use names like Sparky, Rocky, Paul Punk, Happy Hippie, Sally sweetheart, Ralph Redneck, Workingman Williams, Peter Politician, etc. We can call ourselves by any kind of name we want and change it accordingly. Names, therefore, are not that important in regard to our real identity. So who are we?

Not only can we change our names, but we can also change our religion or philosophical viewpoint. We may be Catholic, Protestant, Baptist, Mormon, Amish, Jewish, Muslim, Hindu, Buddhist, or whatever. We may feel very srong towards our particular faith, but we have seen many times how people, for some reasons, give up their faith or may change it. We may be a Buddhist one day and a Hindu the next. Or may we will become an atheist and give up religion altogether. Every individual can change accordingly.

So, what is the difference between one religion and another? It is simply the way we see things and how we want to worship or relate to God. But of what religion is the soul? To what religion does God belong? We may say we are Catholic or Protestant, but does that change the nature of the soul? Does that really change our eternal, spiritual relationship with the Supreme? Therefore on a personal basis, religion, ideals, clothes, names, and even careers, can all be changed as easily as one changes his mind. Yet how does all this affect our real or spiritual identity? How do we really find ourselves and know who are we? What is it that does not change? Even our bodies slowly change from a young body to a middle-aged body, and finally to an old. So who are we?

First of all, let us look at ourselves. Do we really know who or what we are? Maybe not. But take a look at who you think you are. See your hands? Point to them. Now point to your leg. Now your head. Now your stomach. Now point to your heart. Now point to yourself. What are you? Are you the body, mind, or something else?

REVIEW OF WESTERN PHILOSOPHIES

This is a big question that people have been debating for many centuries: is the self separate from the body, or is it a part of the body?

One of the first Western philosophers to consider this was Socrates (469-399 BCE) who believed that the soul was different from the body. He concluded that the soul was released from the body at the time of death, and after death the soul, being immortal and immaterial, would again live in another realm.

Plato (427-347 BCE) also believed that the soul is immortal and unchangeable and exists before the birth and after the demise of the impermanent physical body. But he considered that there are three parts to the soul; one part holds truth and wisdom, another part holds the emotional ambitions and expressions, and the third part consists of the bodily appetites and desires. When all three parts work harmoniously, the individual feels balanced and happy. If one part, say the bodily appetites, are unbalanced or out of control, then life will be frustrating and unsatisfying. Thus, death, wherein the soul attains freedom from the body, becomes a welcome release rather than something to be feared.

Aristotle (384-322 BCE) at first accepted Plato's ideas of the soul but later changed his views. He compared the body to a ship and the soul to its captain, The soul is that which animates the living body. That which has a soul is alive, and that which has no soul is dead. Thus, even animals and plants have source, although they are not developed humans. However, Aristotle did not believe the soul eternal or exist beyond death. Death is the end of the both body and soul. Aristotle's ideas became the basis for thinking that the body and soul are but one mechanism (monism), rather two separate substances working together (dualism).

Later on Descartes (1596-1650), a French philosopher, mathematician, and scientist, propounded the idea of dualism in which he started that the self and body are completely separate. He claimed that there are two kinds of substances; spiritual or mental, and physical. The mind, which is immaterial, immeasurable and invisible, proves its existence by its attribute of thinking: "I think, therefore I am." The physical substance does not think and has no conscious or spiritual attributes.

Descartes proposed that the body and soul work so closely that together they make a whole being and that one can affect the other as when injury to the body creates pain or alarm in the mind. Later in his life, he claimed that the soul must be seated in the pineal gland in the brain because this had to be the link where interaction between the soul and body takes place. However, he could not answer the questions of his contemporaries in regard to how the self, if separate from the body, interacts with the body, or what the mechanism is by which it interacts. He also could not fully explain how conditions of the body affect the mind.

It is obvious that different states of physical condition have an effect on our mind, and because of that it appears that the mind is dependent on the body. When you alter conditions of the brain, the mind is affected, which makes it seem like it is a product of the brain and not independent of it. Since Descartes could not explain this, his ideas ere defeated by other philosophers. So, after Descartes, dualism was not so popular.

Philosophy and science both disputed Descartes notions, and even the Church viewed him as a threat to its authority. In fact, in 1663, the church condemned his books, but by then it was too late. Descartes reasoning helped bring in the Age of Enlightenment in the seventeenth and eighteenth centuries throughout Europe and North America. During this time, the intellectual renaissance challenged the Church's interpretation of social order and opened wide the door to newer philosophies.

Malebranche (1638-1715), another French philosopher, presented the philosophy of occasionalism, in which God came in between the mind and body enabled the two to interact.

A person, or the soul which was separate from the body, would decide to do something, and then God would give the necessary force or mobility. This is very similar to the Vedic concept which we will discuss later. Through Occasionalism the uniting force between the will to act and performing the act was God. But how God was situated in the body and what our relationship was with this localizedfrom of God was not fully explained. So this philosophy was also not conclusive.

Another philosophy introduced was called Interactionism. Interactions try to conceive of the mind as somewhat separate yet somewhat dependent on the body. They try to figure out the cause of the interaction between the mind and brain to explain how the mind was a little bit separate. This is actually the biggest problem in Western philosophy: hoe the mind and body work together but seem to be separate at the same time. In fact, all Western philosophers, including Pythagoras, Plato, Aristotle, and others like David Hume, Immanuel Kant, Georg Hegel, and so on, have all, at some time or other, pondered over this mind/body problem. However, as with Interactionism, they were not able to explain exactly how the mind was separate from the brain.

There were also other philosophers, like Spinoza, who had a big influence on Einstein, and who stated that there was only one substance in all existence. Call it God or matter, it makes no difference, but everything is one and has within it the natural characteristics of consciousness. In other words, according to this idea, atom, molecules, chemicals, etc., are all conscious, and depending on how they were organized would make the difference between lesser or greater consciousness. When they are organized into neurons of the brain, then you would have grater consciousness. Of course, this is absurd because of each cell was conscious of itself, then that consciousness would extend only to an awareness of the other cells around it. So how do all the brain cells develop one collective, integrated consciousness of what exists outside the body? In other words, why am I conscious of others or of experience and memories rather than just neurons beeping around me?So this philosophy is another which does not answer which does not answer the question of how consciousness become integrated.

The point is that as modern science discarded all these philosophies, they were left with nothing but pure mechanism. This meant that every single idea related to consciousness, such as our precipitations, our feelings, experiences, and so on, must all be explained in a mechanism way. In other words, they feel that just by

understanding the neurons in the brain, everything can he explained. This ultimately means that everything is reduced to chemistry: chemicals are the essence of life, and life comes from chemicals. By chemical manipulation, consciousness and everything related to it can be controlled.

It is the same idea in physics, evolution, and the basis or an neurological research and microbiology: that by proper chemical arrangement, as soon as the scientists find out what this is, they will create life. Obviously, with this view in mind, if chemical arrangement must be all there is to consciousness, then through our technology we can recreate consciousness and bring our computers to a stage where they are as good or better than humans.

Very often scientists have a desire t do something that determines or proves the philosophy they use. Rather than simply basing their philosophy on the facts alone, they may trend to base their viewpoints or interpret their experiments on what they desire. In this way, hey may use the idea that life comes from chemicals because if it is true, there are then so many things science can do. With science we could build a better human machine, a better brain, or create immortality. But if it is not true, then science cannot recreate life, or build machines as good as humans, or overcome death. Therefore, science does not want to face that. Instead they may choose to take idea and follow it as far as it will go by using many taxpayers hard-earned dollars to investigate many unless and unnecessary things.

One very famous physicist stated that if there is such a thing as the conscious self, a nonmaterial particle that possesses consciousness which does not come about from chemicals, then scientists might as well retire and become truck drivers. This is an example of the bias in science and the motivation behind rejecting any nonmechanisticidea, and in clinging stubbornly to mechanistic and physical explanations of life. Only in this way can they become like God, with their hopes of creating life and doing so many wonderful things, and denying any need to recognize a Supreme Being.

Today, scientists hardly talk about the mind. They just talk about the brain. There are over a billion neurons in the brain and each of these little brain cells discharge electrical impulses which send out particular kinds of signals. So, the scientists are conceiving of mapping which parts of the brain control cognitive functions, like thinking, memory, motor responses, sensory impressions, etc. Then they hope to stimulate artificially the activity of specific neurons cells with chemicals or electrical shock to negate those neurons that affect one's feelings of anxiety or depressions, or similar unwanted feelings. In this way, one could simply take a chemical in order to feel a particular feelings. This is based on the Western concept thatthe mind is the self and is not separate from the brain, but is a part of it.

The basis of this kind of modern research of the mind was set by the British biologist T.H. Huxley more than century ago. He said that all states of consciousness are caused by molecular changes of the brain. In other words, this is all that causes our changes of mood or the way we feel when experiencing good or bad events in our life. On the basis of this theory, the mind is merely a by-product of a properly functioning brain, and the mind can be controlled simply by adjusting the brin in various ways.

There are, however, a few who do not agree with this. This Australian neurophysiologist and Nobel laureate, Sir john Eccles, thinks that mind or consciousness is separate from the brain. While performing experiments on the cerebral cortex, which controls movements in our bodies by sending appropriate signals to various muscles, he has noted that before any voluntary act is performed, the 50 million or so neurons of the supplementary motor area (SMA) within the cortex begin to act. Thus, the SMA acts before the cerebral cortex sends the necessary signals to the muscles needed to perform the desired activity. Eccles concludes that conscious will, separate from the brain, must first be there before the chain of neurological events begin. Therefore, the mind controls matter rather than matter (the brain) controlling the mind. In this way, we can begin to understand that, as Sir Karl Popper, a philosopher of science, describes, the mind and brain exist in two separate realities. The brain is a functioning material organ of the body, and the mind or consciousness is the immaterial symptom of the living entity or soul which motivates the body, Thus, as explained in the Vedas, the two work together like a driver seated in a car.

PROBLEM WITII SCIENTIFIC THEORIES OF CONSCIOUSNESS

The currents idea that the mind is part of the brain is held not only by many biologists, neurologists, etc., but by others in all branches of science, including physics, computers science, and psychology. We might, however, point out a number of problems with this current thinking. Let us suggest that it is just as reasonable to consider an alternative view, and that the Vedic concept is actually more consistent and does not have as many problems as their concept has.

For example, does a person have the same experience in seeing a sunset as a machine programed to say "I see a red light", when it registers a sunset taking place? In other words, is merely recognizing light eaves all there is to consciousness? If the mind works simply in a mechanistic way, as science tends to propounded, then simply registering that we see a sunset would be all there is to consciousness. It would be exactly like a mechanical reflex to particular stimuli. The point is that we could say a tape recorder hears music, but does it actually hear or enjoy it? Does it get goose bumps or inspiration from listening to it?

The experience of enjoying something cannot be measured or broke down inro a simple mathematical equation. Therefore, in an eliminative or reductionary philosophy, which science used, nit is believed that if something cannot be broken down into a measurable and simple equation, then it is not real and leaves no room for discussion. With this viewpoint, reductionary scientists can begin throwing out a word like "consciousness" because it does not have any meaning or reality. It does not fit into an equation. You can break the movement of brain cells down to a mathematical formula, but not consciousness. And since the word "mind" also does not fit into a equation, we can throw that out as well. And, of course, the concept of a soul has been given up long ago. After all, everything is seen as an extension of the mechanical workings of the brain. So, the idea is that we should only use vocabulary which is related to physical, identifiable, and quantifiable formulas.

By understanding these examples of a machine responding to a red sunset, or a tape recorder hearing music, we can know that there is something in consciousness far beyond the ability of any machine giving simple reactions to external stimuli. Machines reactions are similar to our senses sending electrical message to the brain. But, obviously, we experience more than a simple sensual or physical stimulus. A machine cannot describes the experience of hearing a Beethoven symphony and cannot recognize one piece of music from another. A machine has no emotions, so how can it describe the experience? Therefore, scientists who just try to show that our own responses are a mechanical reaction to sensory stimuli are simple trying to negate the idea of consciousness or the existence of the soul. But, if there is a conscious particle, then they cannot make something else conscious particle or soul, which they cannot do.

From the Vedic literature, we learn that there is a conscious self that is separate from the machine or body. Obviously, we are conscious of every single impulse that the senses of our body/machine deals with. There is perfect interaction. So science will question how the self can interact do well with the machine if it is not part of the machine. And why is consciousness affected when changes are made to the brain? If the self is separate, then consciousness should not be affected. These are the arguments of science, and the Vedic literature offers some very interesting answers. If these arguments are answered, then why not consider an alternative viewpoints, as described in the Vedic literature?

The idea that consciousness is changed by changes of the body or machine can be understood more clearly if we use the example of a person driving car. Obviously, the driver is separate from the car, but if the driver gets in his car and is hit by another car, he will immediately say, "You hit me". It is not that the driver was hit, it was the car that was hit, it was the car that was hit, but the driver identifies with the car, as if he were a part of it. So, the driver is affected by changes in the machine. Similarly, when the self depends on the body and strongly identifies with it, he will think he is the body and will be distributed if there is some problem with it, although he is actually separate from it.

Another example is that there have been carefully controlled and documented experiments done with epileptic patients. In these experiments, the patients have been treated with electric shock to certain parts of the brain in order to respond in a particular way. The findings of these experiments have shown, however, that in almost very case the patient would respond to a certain stimuli stating that he was not doing it, but that the doctor, by controlling the electrical impulses, was making the patient's body respond in a certain way. Thus, the mind's inclination was different or separate from the response of the body. So, simply by applying electric shock to parts of the brain for certain responses does not give any adequate explanations of what is the mind.

In considering the mind, we also have to consider the will. If all that the patients did was respond to stimuli, then, according to the mechanistic theory, that is all that would be expected of being conscious. But the patients were protesting that it was not they who were voluntarily reacting. It was against their will. So, if there were no such things as a separate self with an individual will, there would have been no protest, like a robot programmed to act in a certain way. Therefore, these experiments that showed that the mind had an identity and will separate from the brain were startling is neurological circles. The reason was because it brought up the old arguments that there is something separate between the mind and the brain-it is not all one.

Another example of this is ion the field of near-death experience. They have been top scientists at such places as the University of Virginia using the strictest standards for documenting and researching particular phenomena. They have been able to demonstrative conclusive findings in over hundreds of test cases with patients who were, according to all known laws of physics, technically in a state of unconsciousness, or in a coma due to a heart attack or accident. The patients, after being brought back to consciousness, explained in detail what procedures had been performed to revive them. They describe themselves as floating out of their body, up into the room, looking down and watching the medical procedures the doctors were performing on them. There was no possibility that they could have dreamed this as subsequent tests have shown. This shows that there is a difference between the brain and the mind, and that the mind or consciousness can continue working even though the brain is impaired and hardly functioning at all, as in a comatose state.

In the near-death experience we have the description of what happened to the individuals when they were revived, but what if they had not re-entered their body? What if the patients could not be revived? If they had died, where would they have gone? Or is death simply the end of everything? When someone dies, the relatives may cry and exclaim, "Oh, he is gone, he has left us." But what he is gone? He lying there, or at least the body is. So, if he gone, then it is that part you have not seen that is gone. But what is it?

As we have shown in the last several pages, philosophers and scientists have all questioned this and have arrived at no final conclusion. But the Vedic literature gives detailed descriptions of the self. The Chandogya Upanishad (6.10.3) begins explaining that the subtle essence in all that exists is the self. It is the true and thou art it.

In the Twelfth and Thirteenth Khandas of the Chandogya Upanishad, it gives further examples in which it states that a tall tree has its essence, the self, originally in the small seed from which it grew. Yet, to break a seed open will reveal no such potency for in to grow into such a huge plant. But the power is there. Likewise, to take salt and mix it with water renders the salt invisible; yet, by tasting the water, we can know the salt is there. Similarly, in the material body, the self exists, though we do not directly perceive it. However, Bhagavad-Gita (13.34) explains: "O son of Bharata, as the sun alone illuminates all this universe, so does the living entity, one within the body, illuminate the entire body by consciousness." Therefore, just as we cannot perceive the salt mixed in the water except by recognizing the symptom, which is consciousness.

Consciousness can be recognized easily by performing a small experiment, pinch part of your body and you will fill pain. This is a sign of consciousness not only in humans but also in eats, dogs, or other animals. In any type of species of life, there are two types of bodies; the body which is alive, and the body which is dead and deteriorating. The live body is pervaded and illuminated by the consciousness of the self. The Mundaka Upanishad (3.1.9) says: "The soul is atomic in size and can be perceived by perfect intelligence.

This atomic soul is floating in the five kinds of air (prana, apana, vyana, samana, and udana), is situated within the heart, and spreads its influence all over the body of the embodied living entities. When the soul is purified from the contamination of the five kinds of material air, its spiritual influence is exhibited."

Thus, the self is the motivating factor within the body and when it leaves, the body breaks down and slowly disintegrates. Therefore, the BribadaranyakaUpanishad (2.4.3-5) points out that whomever is dear to us, whether it be our wives, husbands, sons, daughter, teachers, guardians, etc., they are dear to us only due to the presence of the self within the body, who in reality is what is dear to us. Once the self leaves the body, the body becomes unattractive to us because it rapidly gats cold, stiff, and begins to decompose. Therefore, the body is not our real identity, but we are the self within.

THE SOUL IS ETERNAL

The Chandogya Upanishad (6.11.3) also states that although the body withers and dies when the self leaves it, the living self does not die. The Bible also explains: "While we look not at the things which are seen, but at the things which are not seen; for the things which are seen temporal; but the things which are not seen are eternal." (II Corintbians 4:18)

Further enlightenment is given in the Srimad-Bhagavatam (7.2.22): "The spirit soul, the living entity, has no death, for he is eternal and inexhaustible. Being free from material contamination, hc can go anywhcrc in thc material or spiritual worlds. He is fully aware and completely different from the material body, but because of being misled by misuse of his slight independence, he is obliged to accept subtle and gross bodies created by the material energy and thus be subjected to so-called material happiness and distress. Therefore, no ne should lament for the passing of the spirit soul from the body."

The eternal nature of the self is also explained in Bhagavad-Gita by Sri Krishna: "Never was there a time when I did not exist, nor you, nor all these kings; nor in the future shall any of us cease to be. As the embodied soul continually passes, in this body, from boyhood to youth to old age, the soul similarly passes into another body at death. The self-realized soul is not bewildered by such a change." (Bg.2.12-13)

"Know that which pervades the entire body is indestructible. No one is able to destroy the imperishable soul. Only the material body of the indestructible, immeasurable, and eternal living entity is subject to destruction. (Bg.2.17-18)... For the soul there is never birth nor death. Nor, having once been, does he ever cease to be. He is unborn, eternal, ever-existing, undying and primeval. He is not slain when the body is slain. (Bg.2.20)... As a person puts on new garments, giving up old ones, similarly, the soul accepts new material bodies, giving up the old and useless ones." (Bg. 2.23)

Certainly this knowledge can relieve anyone from the anxiety that comes from thinking our existence is finished at death.

Spiritually, we do not die; yet, the body is used until it is no longer fit to continue. At that time, it may appear that we die, but that is not the case. The soul continues on its journey to another body according to its destiny. And if one has sincerely practiced and perfected a genuine spiritual path, then one's next body will not be material, but can be completely spiritual.

Further descriptions of the indestructibility of/ the soul is explained in a way that reveals how it is beyond the influence of all material elements.

"The soul can never be cut into pieces by any weapon, not can he be burned by fire, not withered by the wind. This individual soul is unbreakable and insoluble, and can be neither burned not dried. He is everlasting, all-pervading, unchangeable, immovable and eternally the same. It is said the soul is invisible, immutable, and unchangeable. Knowing this, you should not grieve for the body" (Bg. 2.23.25)

"Some look on the soul as amazing, some describes him as amazing and some hear of him as amazing, while others, even after hearing about him, cannot understand him. at all. O descendent of Bharata, he who dwells in the body is eternal and can never be slain. Therefore you need not grieve for any creature" (Bg.2.29-30)

Let us point out that when it says one should not grieve for any creature, it does not mean that if we see a creature or a person who is suffering that we remain indifferent or callous to the situation. When we see someone who is suffering, we should feel compassion. Compassion is a quality that will make one feel soft-hearted and concerned for the well-being of others. Such a quality is necessary for one who is trying to become fit into the person within. Seeing reality means to recognize the spiritual nature of everyone.

THE VEDIC DESCRIPTION OF THE SOUL

The Srimad-Bhagavtam (11.28.35) explains that the self is self- luminous, beyond birth and death, and unlimited by time or space and, therefore, beyond all changes. The Bhagavatam (11.22.50) also points out that as one witness the birth and death of tree of a tree and is separate from it, similarly the witness of the birth, death, and various activities of the body is separate from it. The Bhagavad-gita also states: "one who can see that all activities are performed by the body, which is created of material nature, and sees that the self does nothing, actually sees. When a sensible man creases to see different identities, which are due to different materials bodies, he attains to the Brahman conception. Thus, he sees that beings are expanded everywhere. Those with the vision of eternity can see that the soul is transcendental, eternal, and beyond the modes of nature. Despite contact with the material body. O Arjuna, the soul neither does anything nor is entangled. The sky, due to its subtle nature, does not mix with anything, although it is all pervading. Similarly, the soul, situated in Brahman vision, does not mix the body, though situated in that body." (Bg.13.30-33)

Although the soul is situated in the body, it is very small and is seated in the heart, according to the Chandogya Upanishad (6.3.3). We can see this since all energy within the body is expanded from the heart. If the heart stop functioning, the whole body collapses. But the heart is simply a seat, which means the seat can be changed as we can observe from heart transplant operations or even from the use of mechanical to receive knowledge of the self. Therefore, we should feel compassion and help resolve the problems of others if we can. But feeling compassion does not mean simply giving hungry people something to eat. Of course, that should be done if we are capable of doing it, but real compassion means helping them understand their real situation and spiritual identity.

For example, as we have explained, the body dwindles and dies but the soul does not die: it simply changes bodies. Therefore, the body is like a shirt or coat which we wear for some time, and when it is worn out, we change it for a new one. So, if we should see someone who is suffering and struggling with material nature, such as a drowning man, what is the use of going out to him and saving only his shirt or coat? We will swim back to shore thinking, "I've saved him," and find that all we have brought back is his shirt, while the real person is still suffering in the ocean of material energy. We must also take care of the person or soul within the shirt or material body. As long as one has a material body, whether in this life or any number of lifetimes after this, there will be so many unavoidable problems, such as birth, disease, old age, and death. Therefore, the Vedic literature, such as the Chandogya Upanishad (8.1.1), mentions that knowledge of the self within is what should be sought and understood by all. Realizing one's spiritual identity solves all the problems of life, as we shall further clarify in this chapter.

The more we realize our spiritual identity, the more we will see that we are beyond these temporary material bodies, and that our identity is not simply being a white body, or black, or yellow, or fat, skinny, intelligent, dumb, old, young, strong, weak, blind, etc. Real blindness means not being able to see through the temporary and superficial bodily conditions and heart. But even with such scientific advancement, if the soul leaves the body, not even a mechanical heart will keep the body functioning for long.

The size of the soul is described in the Svetasvatara Upanishad (5.9): "When the upper point of a hair is divided into one hundred parts and again each of such parts is further divided into one hundred parts, each such part is the measurement of the dimension of the spirit soul."

The Bhagvatam also states: "There are innumerable particles of spiritual atoms, which are measured as one ten-thousandth of the upper portion of the hair." So, obviously, if you take the pinpoint tip of a hair, which usually measures three thousandths of an inch in diameter, and cut it into ten thousand pieces, one such piece will be practically invisible, atomic in size. Therefore, if it takes special equipment to detect the atoms of material substances, it is no wonder that scientific equipment cannot detect atomic particles which are spiritual. Even though scientists want documented proof that there is such a thing as a soul, by studying the Vedic literature, we learn that the soul cannot be observed by ordinary scientific equipment. Of course, as we have established, there are other ways to perceive the soul, especially through the science of yoga and through the study of the Vedic science. We suggest that these scientists study the Vedas to learn about what is beyond their limited sense perception.

The fact is most people have not seen atoms such as protons and neutrons, etc., that scientists talk about. They can only take the word of scientists that such things exist. Similarly, many people have not directly seen the soul. They can only accept the word of those who are supposed to know. But, as previously explained, anyone can recognize the consciousness that pervades the body, the symptom of the soul. This is not difficult. If you pinch or cause some pain to any living entity, whether a person, cat, dog, etc., or approach some wild animal like a bird or squirrel, it will try to get away. This is not some instinctive reflex, but it is due to consciousness. And this is, according to Vedic science, the direct evidence for the existence of the soul, from which consciousness expands through the body.

According to the Vedas, the body is compared to a chariot in which the self is riding. "Transcendentalists who are advanced in knowledge compare the body, which is made by the order of the Supreme Personality of Godhead, to a chariot. The senses are like the horses; the mind, the master of the sense, is like the reins; the objects of the senses are the destinations; intelligence is the chariot driver; and consciousness, which spreads throughout the body, is the cause of bondage in this material world." (Bhag.7.15.41)

In this example, the senses are like horses always pulling the mind towards the object to which they are attracted. The mind is always restless, turbulent, obstinate, and very strong. Only through practice of yoga can the mind be controlled. Otherwise, the mind is always trying to convince the intelligence to make plans to satisfy the senses. In this way, the intelligence, referred to as the chariot driver, will take today here and there in hopes of arriving at the destinations of sense objects, such as nice things to see, taste, feel, hear, and smell. Meanwhile, the self within the body is riding and observing all these activities.

In the KatbaUpanishad (1.3.3-12), which gives the same example, there is further elaboration where it states that he who has no understanding and whose mind (the reins) is never firmly held, his senses (horses) are unmanageable, like vicious horses of a charioteer. But he who has understanding and whose mind is firmly held has senses that are under control like good horses of a charioteer. He who has no understanding enters into the rounds of rebirth; whereas; he who has understanding, who is mindful and pure, reaches that place from whence he is not born again. He reaches the end of his journey, which is the highest adobe of Sri Vishnu in the spiritual atmosphere.

The Katba Upanishad also explains that explains that within the body, higher that the senses and the sense objects, exists the mind. More subtle than the mind is the intelligence, and higher and more subtle than the intellect is the self. That self is hidden in all beings and does not shine forth, but is seen by subtle seers through their sharp intellect.

From this we can understand that within the gross physical body, compared of various material elements, such as earth, air, water, etc., there is also the subtle body composed of the finer subtle elements of mind, intelligence, and ego. The psychic activities take place within the subtle body, and when the unbridled senses and mind are the controllers of a person's goals and desires, much time may be spent in catering to the demands of the mind, or in psychoanalysis with the hopes of calming the mind and figuring out the problems that exists within it. Thus, many people feel that achieving satisfaction of the mind is the goal of life, and then participate in various and sometimes costly programs that promise to accomplish this.

Having the mind pacified may be a relief for anyone who has such mental problems and is looking for a way to relax or sleep better, or lead a happier and healthier life. This is becoming more important to people these days, especially in Western civilization where they may use psychiatric treatments, or take special courses in mind control or hypnosis, or use special subliminal-message tapes to try to get more control over their mind or change their attitude and their life. But this is also one of the purposes of yoga, which has been very effectively practiced for thousands of years. Therefore, Bhagavad-Gita stresses that one must control the lower self by the higher self. The mind will always want to engage in activities of senses gratification and, therefore, must be guided by the intelligence after having cultivated knowledge of the goal of life. The mind absorbed in sense objects is the cause of bondage to material activities, and the mind detached from senses objects is the cause of liberation.

"A person must elevate themselves by their own mind, not degrade themselves. The mid is the friend of the conditioned soul, and enemy as well. For one who has conquered the mind, the mind is the best of friends; but for one who has failed to do so, their very mind can be the greatest enemy." (Bg.6.5-6).

In Bhagavad-Gita, Sri Krishna also advises: "As a lamp in a windless place does not waver, so the transcendentalist, whose mind is controlled, remains always steady in his meditation on the transcendent Self. From whatever and wherever the mind wanders due to its flickering and unsteady nature, one must certainly withdraw it and bring it back under the control of the Self. For one whose mind is unbridled, self-realization is difficult work. But he whose mind is controlled and whose strives by right means is assured of success. That is my opinion." (Bg.6.19,26,36)

In these modern times, however, we see that it is generally recommended that whatever you want to do, if it does not hurt anyone, it is alright. If it feels good, do it. But in the Vedic texts we see that this modern philosophy of allowing the mind to be as free as it can be simply adds fuel to the fire of confusion in society today. By taking advice from Bhagavad-Gita, we can certainly learn how to solve mental problems. These disturbances of the mind are still on a very superficial level because the real self is higher than the mind and the intelligence which can control the mind. Therefore, we have to rise above the subtle elements of mind and intelligence to perceive the self:

"Beyond this gross conception of form [the body] is another, subtle conception of the form [the subtle body or mind, intelligence, and false ego] which is without formal shape and is unseen, unheard, and unmanifest. The living being has his form beyond this subtlety, otherwise he could not have repeated births. Whenever a person experiences, by self-realization, that both the gross and subtle bodies have nothing to do with the pure self, at that time he sees himself as well as the Lord." (Bg.I.3.32-33)

Since we are separate from the gross and subtle bodies, why do we so strongly identify with the material body? This is explained as follows: "Although the material body is different from the self, because of the ignorance of material association one falsely identifies oneself with the superior and inferior bodily conditions. Sometimes a fortunate person is able to give up such mental concoction." (Bhag. I I.22.48)

"The false ego gives shape to illusory material existence and thus experiences material happiness and distress. The spirit soul, however, is transcendental to material nature; he can never actually be affected by material happiness and distress in any place, under any circumstance or by the agency of any persin. A person who understands this has nothing whatsoever to fear from the material creation." (Bhag. I I.23.56)

"No other force besides one's own mental confusion makes the soul experience happiness and distress. His perception of friends, neutral parties and enemies and the whole material life one builds around this perception are simply created out of ignorance." (Bhag. I I.23.59)

In these verses it is clearly explained that only due to the false ego do we think we are the material body, and from such a conception we immediately experience various material desires which cause happiness or distress. There is, however, the sense of real ego, such as, "I am black," "I am white," or thinks they are fat, skinny, short, tall, American, European, Hindu, Muslim, Catholic, Protestant, etc., this is all false ego. It is superficial to our real identity, but this ignorance is the cause of the barriers, quarrels, and misunderstandings between people, communities, neighbors, or nations around the world. However, when the false ego, a product of maya or illusion, which veils the true nature of the self, is cut asunder by the dagger of inquiry into the wisdom of the self, the all-perfect soul then stands reveled. This condition is called the lasting dissolution. Only in this condition will the people of the world ever really experience peace, either individually or on a worldwide basis.

One story that helps elaborate on how the self is separate from the body is found in Srimad-Bhagavatam (Fifth Canto, Chapter Ten), in which a self- realized devotee named Jada Bharata is forced to help carry the palanquin of King Rahugana, who is travelling nearby. The King needs an extra carrier and when the King's man finds Jada Bharata, they force him to help.

The palanquin is not being carried very smoothly and the King, discovering the cause to be Jada Bharata, chastises him very severely. Being very angry, the King says, "You rascal, what are you doing? Are you dead despite the life within your body? Do you not know that I am your master? You are disregarding me and not carrying out my order. For this disobedience I shall now punish you and give you proper treatment so that you will come to your senses and do the correct thing."

Thinking himself a king, King Rahugana is in the bodily conception and is influenced by material nature's mode of passion and ignorance. Due to madness, he chastises Jada Bharata with uncalled for and contradictory words. Jada Bharata is a topmost devotee. Although considering himself very learned, the King does not know about the position of an advanced devotee situated in bhakti-yoga, nor does he know his characteristics. Jada Bharata is the residence of the Supreme Lord; he always carries the form of the Lord within his heart. He is the dear friend of all living beings, and does not entertain any bodily conception. He therefore smiles and speaks the following words:

"My dear king and hero, whatever you have spoken sarcastically is certainly true. Actually, these are not simply words of chastisement, for the body is the carrier. The load carried by the body does not belong to me, for I am the spirit soul. There is no contradiction in your statements because I am different from the body. I am not the carrier of the palanquin; the body is the carrier. Certainly, as you have hinted, I have not labored carrying the palanquin, for I am detached from the body. You have said I am not stout and strong, and these words are benefiting a person who does not know the distinction between the body and soul. The body may be fat or thin, but no learned man would say such things of the spirit soul. As far as the spirit soul is concerned, I am neither fat nor skinny; therefore, you are correct when you say that I am not very stout. Also, if the object of this journey and the path leading there were mine, there would be many troubles for me, but because they relate not to me but to my body, there is no trouble at all.

"Fatness, thinness, bodily and mental distress, thirst, hunger, fear, disagreement, desires for material happiness, old age, sleep, attachment for material possessions, anger, lamentation, illusion and identification of the body with the self are all transformations of the material covering of the spirit soul. A person absorbed in the material bodily conceptions. Consequently, I am neither fat nor skinny nor anything else you have mentioned.

"My dear King, you have unnecessarily accused me of being dead though alive. In this regard, I can only say that this is the case everywhere because everything material has its beginning and end. As far as your thinking that you are a king and master and are thus trying to order me, this is also incorrect because these positions are temporary. Today you are a king and I am your servant, but tomorrow the position may be changed, and you may be my servant and I your master. These are temporary circumstances created by providence. Everyone is being forced into these positions by the laws of material nature; therefore, actually no one is master and no one is servant."

CHAPTER TWENTY

हमारी असली पहचान : आत्मा का वज्ञिञान

इस अध्याय में आध्यात्मकि ज्ञान के संबंध में केछु सबसे मूल्यवान जानकारी है जिसे कोई भी कभी भी पढ़ सकता हौ अगले केछु पन्नों में हम वैदकि प्रमाणों से जीव की वास्तवकि पहचान और प्रकृति को स्थापति करेंगे। केवल यह समझकर कि हम कौन हैं, यह जानन में सक्षम होंगे कि हमें अपने साथ क्या करना है, हम इस दुनयिा में कहां फटि होते हैं, इत्यादि। हम अपने बीच के शारीरकि अंतरों को भी देख पाएंगे और यदि सभी इस ज्ञान को समझ सकें तो हम वश्वि में शांति स्थापति कर सकते हौ लेकनि इस जानकारी को समझे बनिा, इस बात की बहुत कम उम्मीद है कि कभी भी सच्ची शांति मलि पाएगी। इसके अलावा, चाहे आप कसिी भी दर्शन या धर्म की ओर झुके हों, आत्मा के बारे में वसितृत जानकारी को समझे बनिा, आपने जो भी आध्यात्मकि प्रगति की है, व्यावहारकि रूप से बोलना, केवल सतही है और आध्यात्मकि वास्तवकिता की सतह को मुश्कलि से खरोंचता हौ इसलिए, हम सभी को आध्यात्मकि अनुभूति के दूसरे स्तर में प्रवेश करने के लिए इस अध्याय के पाठ्यक्रम का पालन करने के लिए प्रोत्साहति करते हौ

खुद को खोज रहे हैं

दुनयिा के हर हस्सि में लोग इस मामले में काफी हद तक एक जैसे हैं कि हर कोई खुद को खोजने की कोशशि कर रहा हौ फर्क सरिफ इतना है कि वे इसे कैसे करते हौ इस संबंध में, हर कोई केछु हद तक एक दार्शनकि है क्योंकि हर कोई यह पता लगाने की कोशशि कर रहा है कि सुख, मन की

शांति, आदि को पाने के लिए जीवन को कैसे व्यवस्थित किया जाए। लेकिन जब आप अपने आप को खोजने के विचार का उल्लेख करते हैं तो ज्यादातर लोग यह मान लेते हैं कि आप जीवन में सबसे ज्यादा क्या करना चाहते हो। दरअसल, यह केवल मन का विश्लेषण करना है और अपनी पसंद-नापसंद को समझने की कोशिश करना है।

कोई व्यवसायी बनना चाहता है और गगनचुंबी इमारत में एक कार्यालय में नौ से पांच तक काम करना चाहता हो। कोई और प्रसिद्ध फिल्म स्टार बनना चाहता हो। कोई राजनीतिज्ञ, या पुजारी बनना चाहता है, या बस एक व्यापार सीख सकता है और कहीं ग्रामीण इलाकों में परिवार का पालन-पोषण कर सकता हो। एक व्यक्ति अपने आदर्शों के आधार पर बहुत कुछ कर सकता हो।

इन आदर्शों, झुकावों, या प्रवृत्तियों की पहचान करने में, कुछ ऐसे क्लब हो सकते हैं जिनमें हम शामिल होते हैं, या विशिष्ट लोग जिनके साथ हम जुड़ते हैं, या गतिविधियाँ जो हम दूसरों के साथ करते हों। उदाहरण के लिए, जब एक निश्चित स्पोर्ट्स क्लब के प्रशंसक, जैसे फुटबॉल या बेसबॉल में, अपनी पसंदीदा टीम को खेलते हुए देखने जाते हैं, तो वे टीम की वर्दी के समान रंग पहन सकते हों या वे एक प्रतीक के साथ टोपी या शर्ट जैसी कोई चीज पहन सकते हैं जो टीम के प्रति उनकी वफादारी का प्रतीक हो। वे टीम के लिए चीयर करते हैं, शायद उनके लिए लड़ते भी हैं और अगर टीम जीतती है तो वे खुशी और गर्व महसूस करते हैं और अन्य प्रशंसकों के साथ जश्न मनाएंगे।

युवा लोग विशिष्ट रूप से विशिष्ट आदर्शों की पहचान करने और उन्हें व्यक्तिगत रूप से अभिव्यक्त करने में बहुत अधिक ऊर्जा लगा सकते हों। वे कुछ कपड़े और केश-विन्यास पहन सकते हैं, एक विशिष्ट प्रकार का संगीत सुन सकते हैं, और क्लबों में समान रुचि रखने वाले दोस्तों से मिल सकते हैं जो उनकी पसंद को पूरा करते हों। वे अपने आदर्शों को दूसरों तक प्रचारित करने में भी संलग्न हो सकते हों। यह सब हमारी भौतिक पहचान को खोजने की कोशिश का हिस्सा हो।

अगर, हालांकि, हम अपनी खुद की पहचान नहीं पा सकते हैं, तो हम खुद को किसी विशिष्ट हस्ती के फैशन में ढाल सकते हैं, जिसकी हम प्रशंसा करते हैं। हम उनके जैसे कपड़े पहन सकते हैं, उनकी तरह बात कर सकते हैं, जैसे वे करते हैं, आदि। लेकिन जैसे-जैसे हम बड़े होते हैं, हम अपने काम करने के तरीके को बदल सकते हैं। हो सकता है कि हम पहले की तरह अजीबोगरीब कपड़े न पहनें, या अपने बालों को लंबे समय तक रखें, या देर तक बाहर रहें। तो हम कौन हैं? इनमें से कौन सी पहचान वास्तविक हम हैं? जैसे आदर्श परिवर्तनशील होते हैं, वैसे ही हमारे नाम भी परिवर्तनशील होते हैं। हम खुद को कुछ खास नामों से बुला सकते हैं, या तो आवश्यकता से बाहर, जैसे कि परिवार का नाम, या व्यक्तित्व के लिए, जैसे कि कुछ मनोरंजनकर्ता उपयोग करते हैं। हम खुद को रॉबर्ट या रोबर्टा, स्टीफन या स्टेफनी, हेनरी या हेनरीटा कह सकते हैं। या हम स्पार्की, रॉकी, पॉल पंक, हैप्पी हिप्पी, सैली स्वीटहार्ट, राल्फ रेडनेक, वर्किंगमैन विलियम्स, पीटर पॉलिटिशियिन आदि जैसे नामों का उपयोग कर सकते हैं। इसलिए, नाम हमारी वास्तविक पहचान के संबंध में उतने महत्वपूर्ण नहीं हैं। तो हम कौन हैं?

न केवल हम अपना नाम बदल सकते हैं, बल्कि हम अपना धर्म या दार्शनिक दृष्टिकोण भी बदल सकते हैं। हम कैथोलिक, प्रोटेस्टेंट, बैपटिस्ट, मॉर्मन, अमीश, यहूदी, मुसलिम, हिंदू, बौद्ध, या जो कुछ भी हो सकते हैं। हम अपने धर्म विशिष्ट के प्रति बहुत कठोर महसूस कर सकते हैं, लेकिन हमने कई बार देखा है कि कैसे लोग किन्हीं कारणों से अपनी आस्था को छोड़ देते हैं या इसे बदल सकते हैं। हम एक दिन बौद्ध और दूसरे दिन हिंदू हो सकते हैं या हो सकता है कि हम नास्तिक बन जाएं और धर्म को पूरी तरह छोड़ दें। प्रत्येक व्यक्ति तदनुसार बदल सकता है।

तो, एक धर्म और दूसरे धर्म में क्या अंतर है? यह केवल वह तरीका है जिससे हम चीजों को देखते हैं और हम किस तरह से भगवान की पूजा करना या उससे संबंधित होना चाहते हैं। लेकिन आत्मा किस धर्म की है? भगवान किस धर्म से संबंध रखते हैं? हम कह सकते हैं कि हम कैथोलिक या प्रोटेस्टेंट हैं, लेकिन क्या इससे आत्मा का स्वभाव बदल जाता है? क्या

यह वास्तव में परमेश्वर के साथ हमारे शाश्वत, आध्यात्मिक संबंध को बदल देता है? इसलिए व्यक्तिगत आधार पर, धर्म, आदर्श, कपड़े, नाम और यहां तक कि करियर, सब कुछ हो सकता है जितनी आसानी से कोई अपना मन बदलता है उतनी ही आसानी से बदल जाता है। फिर भी यह सब हमारी वास्तविक या आध्यात्मिक पहचान को कैसे प्रभावित करता है? हम वास्तव में अपने आप को कैसे पाते हैं और जानते हैं कि हम कौन हैं? ऐसा क्या है जो नहीं बदलता? यहां तक कि हमारे शरीर भी धीरे-धीरे एक युवा शरीर से एक मध्यम आयु के शरीर में और अंत में एक बूढ़े शरीर में बदलते हों तो हम कौन हैं?

सबसे पहले हम अपने आप को देखें। क्या हम वास्तव में जानते हैं कि हम कौन हैं या क्या हैं? शायद नहीं। लेकिन जरा गौर कीजिए कि आप अपने बारे में क्या सोचते हैं। अपने हाथ देखें? उनकी ओर इशारा करें अब अपने पैर की ओर इशारा करें अब तुम्हारा सिर। अब आपका पेट। अब अपने दिल की ओर इशारा करें अब अपनी ओर इशारा करें तुम क्या हो? क्या आप शरीर हैं, मन हैं, या कुछ और हैं?

पश्चिमी दर्शन की समीक्षा

यह एक बड़ा सवाल है जिस पर सदियों से लोग बहस करते आ रहे हैं: क्या आत्मा शरीर से अलग है, या यह शरीर का एक हिस्सा है?

इस पर विचार करने वाले पहले पश्चिमी दार्शनिकों में से एक सुकरात (469-399 ईसा पूर्व) थे जो मानते थे कि आत्मा शरीर से अलग थी। उन्होंने निष्कर्ष निकाला कि मृत्यु के समय आत्मा को शरीर से मुक्त कर दिया गया था, और मृत्यु के बाद आत्मा, अमर और अभौतिक होने के कारण, फिर से दूसरे क्षेत्र में रहेगी।

प्लेटो (427-347 ईसा पूर्व) का भी मानना था कि आत्मा अमर और अपरिवर्तनीय है और जन्म से पहले और नश्वर भौतिक शरीर के निधन के बाद मौजूद है। लेकिन उन्होंने माना कि आत्मा के तीन भाग हैं; एक भाग सत्य और ज्ञान को धारण करता है, दूसरा भाग भावनात्मक महत्वाकांक्षाओं और अभिव्यक्तियों को धारण करता है, और तीसरे भाग में शारीरिक भूख और इच्छाएँ होती हैं। जब तीनों अंग सामंजस्यपूर्ण रूप

से काम करते हैं, तो व्यक्ति संतुलित और खुश महसूस करता हो यदि एक भाग, जैसे शारीरिक भूख, असंतुलित या नियंत्रण से बाहर हो, तो जीवन निराशाजनक और असंतोषजनक होगा। इस प्रकार, मृत्यु, जिसमें आत्मा शरीर से मुक्ति प्राप्त करती हो, भयभीत होने के बजाय एक स्वागत योग्य मुक्ति बन जाती हो

अरस्तू (384-322 ईसा पूर्व) ने पहले प्लेटो के आत्मा के विचारों को स्वीकार किया लेकिन बाद में अपने विचारों को बदल दिया। उन्होंने शरीर की तुलना एक जहाज से और आत्मा की उसके कप्तान से की, आत्मा वह हो जो जीवित शरीर को अनुप्राणित करती हो जिसके पास आत्मा है वह जीवित है, और जिसमें आत्मा नहीं है वह मर चुका हो इस प्रकार, यहां तक कि जानवरों और पौधों का भी स्रोत हो, हालांकि वे विकसित मानव नहीं हो हालाँकि, अरस्तू विश्वास नहीं करता था कि आत्मा शाश्वत है या मृत्यु से परे मौजूद हो मृत्यु शरीर और आत्मा दोनों का अंत हो अरस्तू के विचार यह सोचने का आधार बन गए कि शरीर और आत्मा एक तंत्र (अद्वैतवाद) हैं, बल्कि दो अलग-अलग पदार्थ एक साथ काम कर रहे हैं (द्वैतवाद)।

बाद में डेसकार्ट्स (1596-1650), एक फ्रांसीसी दार्शनिक, गणितिज्ञ और वैज्ञानिक ने द्वैतवाद के विचार को प्रतिपादित किया जिसमें उन्होंने शुरू किया कि आत्म और शरीर पूरी तरह से अलग हो उन्होंने दावा किया कि पदार्थ दो प्रकार के होते हैं; आध्यात्मिक या मानसिक, और शारीरिक। मन, जो कि अमूर्त, अथाह और अदृश्य है, अपनी सोच की विशेषता से अपने अस्तित्व को सिद्ध करता है: "मैं सोचता हूँ इसलिए मैं हूँ" भौतिक पदार्थ सोचता नहीं है और इसमें कोई सचेतन या आध्यात्मिक विशेषताएँ नहीं हो

डेसकार्ट्स ने प्रस्तावित किया कि शरीर और आत्मा इतनी निकटता से काम करते हैं कि वे एक साथ मिलकर एक संपूर्ण अस्तित्व बनाते हैं और यह कि एक दूसरे को प्रभावित कर सकता है जैसे कि शरीर पर चोट लगने से मन में दर्द या अलार्म पैदा होता हो बाद में अपने जीवन में, उन्होंने दावा किया कि आत्मा को मस्तिष्क में पीनियल ग्रंथि में बैठा होना चाहिए

क्योंकि यह वह कड़ी थी जहां आत्मा और शरीर के बीच परस्पर क्रिया होती है। हालांकि, वह अपने समकालीनों के सवालों का जवाब नहीं दे सका कि आत्मा, अगर शरीर से अलग है, शरीर के साथ कैसे संपर्क करता है, या वह तंत्र क्या है जिसके द्वारा यह बातचीत करता है। वह यह भी पूरी तरह से नहीं बता सके कि शरीर की स्थितियां मन को कैसे प्रभावित करती हैं।

यह स्पष्ट है कि शरीर की भिन्न-भिन्न अवस्थाओं का हमारे मन पर प्रभाव पड़ता है और उसके कारण ऐसा प्रतीत होता है कि मन शरीर पर निर्भर है। जब आप मस्तिष्क की स्थितियों को बदलते हैं, तो मन प्रभावित होता है, जिससे ऐसा लगता है कि यह मस्तिष्क का एक उत्पाद है और इससे स्वतंत्र नहीं है। चूंकि डेसकार्टेस इसकी व्याख्या नहीं कर सका, उसके विचार अन्य दार्शनिकों द्वारा पराजित हो गए। इसलिए, डेसकार्टेस के बाद, द्वैतवाद इतना लोकप्रिय नहीं था।

दर्शनशास्त्र और विज्ञान दोनों ने डेसकार्टेस की धारणाओं पर विवाद किया, और यहां तक कि चर्च ने भी उसे अपने अधिकार के लिए खतरे के रूप में देखा। वास्तव में, 1663 में, चर्च ने उनकी पुस्तकों की निंदा की, लेकिन तब तक बहुत देर हो चुकी थी। डेसकार्टेस के तर्क ने पूरे यूरोप और उत्तरी अमेरिका में सत्रहवीं और अठारहवीं शताब्दी में ज्ञानोदय के युग को लाने में मदद की। इस समय के दौरान, बौद्धिक पुनर्जागरण ने चर्च की सामाजिक व्यवस्था की व्याख्या को चुनौती दी और नए दर्शन के लिए दरवाजे खोल दिए।

मालेब्रंच (1638-1715), एक अन्य फ्रांसीसी दार्शनिक, ने सामयिकवाद के दर्शन को प्रस्तुत किया, जिसमें ईश्वर मन और शरीर के बीच में आया और दोनों को बातचीत करने में सक्षम बनाया।

एक व्यक्ति, या आत्मा जो शरीर से अलग थी, कुछ करने का फैसला करेगी, और फिर भगवान आवश्यक शक्ति या गतिशीलता देंगे। यह वैदिक अवधारणा से काफी मिलता-जुलता है जिसकी चर्चा हम बाद में करेंगे। अवसरवाद के माध्यम से कार्य करने की इच्छा और कार्य करने के बीच एक्जिक्यूट करने वाली शक्ति ईश्वर थी। लेकिन भगवान कैसे सत्तिआ थे शरीर में टेड और भगवान के इस स्थानीय रूप से हमारा क्या संबंध था, यह पूरी

तरह से समझाया नहीं गया था। अतः यह दर्शन भी निर्णायक नहीं था।

पेश किए गए एक अन्य दर्शन को अंतःक्रियावाद कहा जाता था। अंतःक्रिया मन को कुछ हद तक अलग लेकिन कुछ हद तक शरीर पर निर्भर करने की कल्पना करने की कोशिश करती है। वे यह समझाने की कोशिश करते हैं कि मन और मस्तिष्क के बीच की बातचीत का कारण यह है कि मन थोड़ा अलग कैसे था। यह वास्तव में पश्चिमी दर्शन में सबसे बड़ी समस्या है: कैसे मन और शरीर एक साथ काम करते हैं लेकिन एक ही समय में अलग प्रतीत होते हैं। वास्तव में, पाइथागोरस, प्लेटो, अरस्तू और अन्य जैसे डेविड ह्यूम, इमैनुएल कांट, जॉर्ज हेगेल और अन्य सहित सभी पश्चिमी दार्शनिकों ने, किसी न किसी समय, इस मन/शरीर की समस्या पर विचार किया है। हालाँकि, अंतःक्रियावाद की तरह, वे ठीक से यह समझाने में सक्षम नहीं थे कि मन मस्तिष्क से अलग कैसे था।

स्पिनोजा जैसे अन्य दार्शनिक भी थे, जिनका आइंस्टीन पर बड़ा प्रभाव था, और जिन्होंने कहा कि सभी अस्तित्व में केवल एक ही पदार्थ है। इसे ईश्वर कहें या पदार्थ, इससे कोई फर्क नहीं पड़ता, लेकिन सब कुछ एक है और इसके भीतर चेतना की स्वाभाविक विशेषताएं हैं। दूसरे शब्दों में, इस विचार के अनुसार, परमाणु, अणु, रसायन आदि सभी सचेतन हैं, और वे कैसे संगठित थे, इस पर निर्भर करते हुए वे कम या अधिक चेतना के बीच अंतर करेंगे। जब वे मस्तिष्क के न्यूरॉन्स में व्यवस्थित होते हैं, तब आपके पास अधिक चेतना होगी। बेशक, यह बेतुका है क्योंकि प्रत्येक कोशिका स्वयं के प्रति सचेत थी, फिर वह चेतना केवल अपने आसपास की अन्य कोशिकाओं के प्रति जागरूकता तक ही विस्तारित होगी। तो मस्तिष्क की सभी कोशिकाएं एक सामूहिक, एकीकृत चेतना कैसे विकसित करती हैं जो शरीर के बाहर मौजूद है? दूसरे शब्दों में, मैं दूसरों के बारे में या अनुभव और यादों के बारे में क्यों सचेत हूं, न कि मेरे चारों ओर सिर्फ न्यूरॉन्स की आवाज?

मुद्दा यह है कि जैसे-जैसे आधुनिक विज्ञान ने इन सभी दर्शनों को त्याग दिया, उनके पास शुद्ध तंत्र के अलावा कुछ नहीं बचा। इसका मतलब यह था कि चेतना से संबंधित हर एक विचार, जैसे कि हमारी

अवक्षेपण, हमारी भावनाएं, अनुभव, और इसी तरह, सभी को एक तंत्र तरीके से समझाया जाना चाहिए। दूसरे शब्दों में, वे महसूस करते हैं कि बिस द्वारा

मस्तिष्क में न्यूरॉन्स को समझकर, वह सब कुछ समझा सकता हो अंततः इसका मतलब यह है कि सब कुछ रसायन शास्त्र में सिमट गया है: रसायन जीवन का सार हैं, और जीवन रसायनों से आता हो रासायनिक हेरफेर से चेतना और उससे जुड़ी हर चीज को नियंत्रित किया जा सकता हो

भौतिकी, विकास, और आधार या एक न्यूरोलॉजिकल शोध और सूक्ष्म जीव विज्ञान में यह एक ही विचार है: कि उचित रासायनिक व्यवस्था द्वारा, जैसे ही वैज्ञानिकों को पता चलेगा कि यह क्या है, वे जीवन का निर्माण करेंगे। जाहिर है, इस विचार को ध्यान में रखते हुए, अगर चेतना के लिए रासायनिक व्यवस्था ही सब कुछ होनी चाहिए, तो हम अपनी तकनीक के माध्यम से चेतना को फिर से बना सकते हैं और अपने कंप्यूटर को एक ऐसी स्थिति में ला सकते हैं जहां वे इंसानों की तुलना में अच्छे या बेहतर हो।

बहुत बार वैज्ञानिकों की इच्छा होती है कि वे कुछ ऐसा करें जो उनके द्वारा उपयोग किए जाने वाले दर्शन को निर्धारित या सिद्ध करो अपने दर्शन को केवल तथ्यों पर आधारित करने के बजाय, वे अपने दृष्टिकोण को आधार बनाने या अपनी इच्छा के अनुसार अपने प्रयोगों की व्याख्या करने के लिए प्रवृत्त हो सकते हों इस तरह, वे इस विचार का उपयोग कर सकते हैं कि जीवन रसायनों से आता है क्योंकि अगर यह सच है, तो ऐसी बहुत सी चीजें हैं जो विज्ञान कर सकता हो विज्ञान के साथ हम एक बेहतर मानव मशीन, एक बेहतर मस्तिष्क या अमरता का निर्माण कर सकते हों लेकिन अगर यह सच नहीं है, तो विज्ञान जीवन को फिर से नहीं बना सकता है, न ही इंसानों जैसी मशीनों का निर्माण कर सकता है, या मृत्यु पर काबू पा सकता हो इसलिए विज्ञान इसका सामना नहीं करना चाहता। इसके बजाय वे विचार लेना चुन सकते हैं और इसका पालन कर सकते हैं जहां तक यह कई करदाताओं की मेहनत से कमाए गए डॉलर का उपयोग करके कई अनावश्यक और अनावश्यक चीजों की जांच कर सकता हो

एक बहुत प्रसिद्ध भौतिक वैज्ञानी ने कहा कि अगर चेतन स्व जैसी कोई चीज है, एक गैर-भौतिक कण जिसमें चेतना है जो रसायनों से नहीं आती है, तो वैज्ञानिक संवानवितृत हो सकते हैं और ट्रक चालक बन सकते हैं। यह विज्ञान में पूर्वाग्रह का एक उदाहरण है और किसी भी गैर-यांत्रिकी विचार को खारिज करने के पीछे की प्रेरणा, और जीवन की यंत्रवत और भौतिक व्याख्याओं पर अडिग रहने का एक उदाहरण है। केवल इसी तरह से वे ईश्वर के समान बन सकते हैं, जीवन की रचना करने की अपनी आशाओं के साथ और इतने सारे अद्भुत काम करने के साथ, और एक सर्वोच्च व्यक्ति को पहचानने की किसी भी आवश्यकता से इनकार करते हुए।

आज वैज्ञानिक शायद ही मन के बारे में बात करते हैं। वे सिर्फ दिमाग की बात करते हैं। मस्तिष्क में एक अरब से अधिक न्यूरॉन्स होते हैं और इनमें से प्रत्येक छोटी मस्तिष्क कोशिकाएं विद्युत आवेगों का निर्वहन करती हैं जो विशिष्ट प्रकार के संकेत भेजते हैं। इसलिए, वैज्ञानिक मानचित्रण की कल्पना कर रहे हैं कि मस्तिष्क के कौन से हिस्से संज्ञानात्मक कार्यों को नियंत्रित करते हैं, जैसे कि सोच, स्मृति, मोटर प्रतिक्रियाएं, संवेदी छापें, आदि। फिर वे कृत्रिम रूप से विशिष्ट न्यूरॉन्स कोशिकाओं की गतिविधि को रसायनों या बिजली के झटके से उत्तेजित करने की उम्मीद करते हैं ताकि उन्हें नकारा जा सके। न्यूरॉन्स जो प्रभावित करते हैं किसी की चिंता या अवसाद, या इसी तरह की अवांछित भावनाओं की भावनाएँ। इस तरह, एक विशिष्ट भावना को महसूस करने के लिए कोई भी केवल एक रसायन ले सकता है। यह पश्चिमी अवधारणा पर आधारित है कि मन स्वयं है और मस्तिष्क से अलग नहीं है, बल्कि इसका एक हिस्सा है।

मस्तिष्क के इस प्रकार के आधुनिक शोध का आधार ब्रिटिश जीवविज्ञानी टी.एच. हक्सले सदी से भी पहले। उन्होंने कहा कि चेतना की सभी अवस्थाएं मस्तिष्क के आणविक परिवर्तनों के कारण होती हैं। दूसरे शब्दों में, यह वह सब है जो हमारे मूड के परिवर्तन का कारण बनता है या जिस तरह से हम अपने जीवन में अच्छी या बुरी घटनाओं का

अनुभव करते हैं। इस सिद्धांत के आधार पर, मन ठीक से काम करने वाले मस्तिष्क का एक उप-उत्पाद मात्र है, और मस्तिष्क को विभिन्न तरीकों से समायोजित करके मन को नियंत्रित किया जा सकता है।

हालांकि कुछ ऐसे भी हैं जो इससे इत्तेफाक नहीं रखते। यह ऑस्ट्रेलियाई न्यूरोफजियोलॉजिस्ट और नोबेल पुरस्कार विजेता सर जॉन एक्लस सोचते हैं कि मन या चेतना मस्तिष्क से अलग है। सेरेब्रल कॉर्टेक्स पर प्रयोग करते हुए, जो विभिन्न मांसपेशियों को उचित संकेत भेजकर हमारे शरीर में आंदोलनों को नियंत्रित करता है, उन्होंने नोट किया है कि किसी भी स्वैच्छिक कार्य को करने से पहले, कॉर्टेक्स के भीतर पूरक मोटर क्षेत्र (SMA) के 50 मिलियन या इतने ही न्यूरॉन्स अभिनय करना शुरू करो। इस प्रकार, सेरेब्रल कॉर्टेक्स वांछित गतिविधि करने के लिए आवश्यक मांसपेशियों को आवश्यक संकेत भेजने से पहले SMA कार्य करता है। सभोपदेशक का निष्कर्ष है कि मस्तिष्क से अलग चेतन इच्छा, स्नायविक घटनाओं की श्रृंखला शुरू होने से पहले पहल होनी चाहिए। इसलिए, पदार्थ (मस्तिष्क) मन को नियंत्रित करने के बजाय मन पदार्थ को नियंत्रित करता है। इस तरह, हम यह समझना शुरू कर सकते हैं कि, जैसा कि सर कार्ल पॉपर, विज्ञान के एक दार्शनिक वर्णन करते हैं, मन और मस्तिष्क दो अलग-अलग वास्तविकताओं में मौजूद हैं। मस्तिष्क शरीर का एक सक्रिय भौतिक अंग है, और मन या चेतना जीव या आत्मा का अभौतिक लक्षण है जो शरीर को प्रेरित करता है, इस प्रकार, जैसा कि वेदों में बताया गया है, दोनों कार में बैठे ड्राइवर की तरह एक साथ काम करते हैं .

चेतना के वैज्ञानिक सिद्धांतों के साथ समस्या

धाराओं का विचार है कि दिमाग मस्तिष्क का हिस्सा है, न केवल कई जीवविज्ञानी, न्यूरोलॉजिस्ट इत्यादि द्वारा आयोजित किया जाता है, बल्कि भौतिकी, कंप्यूटर विज्ञान और मनोविज्ञान समेत विज्ञान की सभी शाखाओं में अन्य लोगों द्वारा आयोजित किया जाता है। हालाँकि, हम इस वर्तमान सोच के साथ कई समस्याओं की ओर इशारा कर सकते हैं। आइए हम सुझाव दें कि वैकल्पिक दृष्टिकोण पर विचार करना उतना ही

उचति हैं, और यह कि वैदकि अवधारणा वास्तव में अधकि ससुंगत हैं और इसमें उतनी समस्याएँ नहीं हैं जतिनी कि उनकी अवधारणा में हैं।

उदाहरण के लिए, क्या किसी व्यक्ति को सूर्यास्त देखने का वैसा ही अनुभव होता हैं जैसा किसी मशीन को प्रोग्राम करके कहा जाता हैं कि "मुझे एक लाल बत्ती दिखाई देती हैं", जब वह सूर्यास्त दर्ज करती हैं? दूसरे शब्दों में, क्या चेतना के लिए केवल प्रकाश छज्जों को पहचानना ही सब कुछ हैं? यदि मन यंत्रवत तरीके से काम करता हैं, जैसा कि विज्ञान प्रतिपादति करता हैं, तो बस यह दर्ज करना कि हम सूर्यास्त देखते हैं, चेतना के लिए सब कुछ होगा। यह बलिकुल विशिष उत्तेजनाओं के लिए एक यांत्रकि प्रतविर्त जैसा होगा। मुद्दा यह हैं कि हम कह सकते हैं कि एक टेप रकिॉर्डर संगीत सुनता हैं, लेकनि क्या यह वास्तव में इसे सुनता हैं या इसका आनंद लेता हैं? इसे सुनकर रोगंटे खड़े हो जाते हैं या प्रेरणा मलिती हैं?

किसी चीज़ का आनंद लेने के अनुभव को एक साधारण गणतिीय समीकरण में नापा या तोड़ा नहीं जा सकता। इसलिए, एक वलिोपन या न्यूनीकरण दर्शन में, जसिका वज्ञिान उपयोग करता हैं, यह माना जाता हैं कि यदि किसी चीज़ को मापने योग्य और सरल समीकरण में तोड़ा नहीं जा सकता हैं, तो यह वास्तवकि नहीं हैं और चर्चा के लिए कोई जगह नहीं छोड़ता हौ। इस दृष्टकिोण के साथ, कमी करने वाले वैज्ञानकि "चेतना" जैसे शब्द को फेंकना शुरू कर सकते हैं क्योंकि इसका कोई अर्थ या वास्तवकिता नहीं हौ। यह एक समीकरण में फटि नहीं होता हौ। आप मस्तष्कि की कोशकिाओं की गतकि को एक गणतिीय सूत्र तक तोड़ सकते हैं, लेकनि चेतना को नहीं। और चूंकि "मन" शब्द भी किसी समीकरण में फटि नहीं बैठता हैं, तो हम उसे भी बाहर नकिाल सकते हौ और नश्चिति रूप से आत्मा की अवधारणा बहुत पहले छोड़ दी गई हौ। आखरिकार, हर चीज को मस्तष्कि की यांत्रकि कार्यप्रणाली के वसि्तार के रूप में देखा जाता हौ। तो, वचिार यह हैं कि हमें केवल ऐसी शब्दावली का उपयोग करना चाहिए जो भौतकि, पहचान योग्य और मात्रात्मक सूत्रों से संबंधति हो।

लाल सूर्यास्त पर प्रतिक्रिया देने वाली मशीन, या संगीत सुनने वाले टेप रिकॉर्डर के इन उदाहरणों को समझकर, हम जान सकते हैं कि बाहरी उत्तेजनाओं को सरल प्रतिक्रिया देने वाली किसी भी मशीन की क्षमता से परे चेतना में कुछ है। मशीनों की प्रतिक्रियाएं मस्तिष्क को विद्युत संदेश भेजने वाली हमारी इंद्रियों के समान होती हैं लेकिन, जाहिर है, हम एक साधारण कामुक या शारीरिक उत्तेजना से अधिक अनुभव करते हैं। एक मशीन बीथोवेन सिम्फनी सुनने के अनुभव का वर्णन नहीं कर सकती है और संगीत के एक टुकड़े को दूसरे से नहीं पहचान सकती है। एक मशीन में कोई भावना नहीं होती, तो वह अनुभव का वर्णन कैसे कर सकती है? इसलिए, वैज्ञानिक जो सिर्फ यह दिखाने की कोशिश करते हैं कि हमारी अपनी प्रतिक्रियाएँ संवेदी उत्तेजनाओं के लिए एक यांत्रिक प्रतिक्रिया हैं, वे चेतना या आत्मा के अस्तित्व के विचार को नकारने की कोशिश कर रहे हैं। लेकिन, अगर कोई सचेत हिस्सा है अगर, तो वे कुछ और चेतन कण या आत्मा नहीं बना सकते, जो वे नहीं कर सकते।

वैदिक साहित्य से, हम सीखते हैं कि एक चेतन आत्मा है जो मशीन या शरीर से अलग है। जाहिर है, हम हर उस आवेग के प्रति सचेत हैं जिससे हमारे शरीर/मशीन की इंद्रियां निपटती हैं। परफेक्ट इंटरेक्शन है। तो विज्ञान सवाल करेगा कि अगर मशीन का हिस्सा नहीं है तो स्वयं मशीन के साथ अच्छी तरह से कैसे बातचीत कर सकता है। और मस्तिष्क में परिवर्तन होने पर चेतना क्यों प्रभावित होती है? यदि आत्मा अलग है, तो चेतना प्रभावित नहीं होनी चाहिए। ये विज्ञान के तर्क हैं, और वैदिक साहित्य कुछ बहुत ही रोचक उत्तर प्रदान करता है। यदि इन तर्कों का उत्तर दिया जाता है, तो क्यों न एक वैकल्पिक दृष्टिकोण पर विचार किया जाए, जैसा कि वैदिक साहित्य में वर्णित है?

यह विचार कि चेतना शरीर या मशीन के परिवर्तनों से बदल जाती है, अधिक स्पष्ट रूप से समझा जा सकता है यदि हम कार चलाने वाले व्यक्ति के उदाहरण का उपयोग करते हैं। जाहिर है, ड्राइवर कार से अलग है, लेकिन अगर ड्राइवर अपनी कार में बैठ जाता है और दूसरी कार से टकरा जाता है, तो वह तुरंत कहेगा, "तुमने मुझे मारा"। ऐसा नहीं है कि चालक को

टक्कर मारी गई थी, वह कार थी जिसे टक्कर मारी गई थी, वह कार थी जिसे टक्कर मारी गई थी, लेकिन चालक कार से पहचान करता है, जैसे कि वह उसका एक हिस्सा हो। तो, मशीन में परिवर्तन से चालक प्रभावित होता है। इसी प्रकार, जब आत्म शरीर पर निर्भर करता है और इसके साथ दृढ़ता से पहचान करता है, तो वह सोचेगा कि वह शरीर है और इसमें कुछ समस्या होने पर विचरित किया जाएगा, हालांकि वह वास्तव में इससे अलग है।

एक अन्य उदाहरण यह है कि मिरगी के रोगियों के साथ सावधानीपूर्वक नियंत्रित और प्रलेखित प्रयोग किए गए हैं। इन प्रयोगों में, एक विशिष्ट तरीके से प्रतिक्रिया करने के लिए रोगियों को मस्तिष्क के कुछ हिस्सों में बिजली के झटके से इलाज किया गया है। हालांकि, इन प्रयोगों के निष्कर्षों से पता चला है कि लगभग बहुत ही मामलों में रोगी एक निश्चित उत्तेजना का जवाब देगा, यह कहते हुए कि वह ऐसा नहीं कर रहा था, लेकिन डॉक्टर विद्युत आवेगों को नियंत्रित करके, रोगी के शरीर को एक तरह से प्रतिक्रिया दे रहा था। निश्चित तरीका। इस प्रकार मन का झुकाव शरीर की प्रतिक्रिया से अलग या अलग था। तो, केवल कुछ प्रतिक्रियाओं के लिए मस्तिष्क के कुछ हिस्सों में बिजली के झटके लगाने से मन क्या है, इसकी कोई पर्याप्त व्याख्या नहीं होती है।

मन पर विचार करते हुए हमें इच्छा पर भी विचार करना होगा। यदि रोगियों ने जो कुछ भी किया वह उत्तेजनाओं का जवाब था, तो यंत्रवत सिद्धांत के अनुसार, जागरूक होने की उम्मीद की जा सकती है। लेकिन मरीज विरोध कर रहे थे कि यह वे नहीं थे जो स्वेच्छा से प्रतिक्रिया कर रहे थे। यह उनकी इच्छा के विरुद्ध था। इसलिए, यदि व्यक्तिगत इच्छा के साथ एक अलग स्व जैसी कोई चीज नहीं होती, तो कोई विरोध नहीं होता, जैसे एक रोबोट को एक निश्चित तरीके से कार्य करने के लिए प्रोग्राम किया गया हो। इसलिए, ये प्रयोग जो दिखाते हैं कि दिमाग की एक पहचान थी और मस्तिष्क से अलग हो जाएगा, चौंकाने वाला स्नायु मंडल है। कारण यह था कि इसने पुराने तर्कों को जन्म दिया कि मन और मस्तिष्क के बीच कुछ अलग है—यह सब एक नहीं है।

इसका एक अन्य उदाहरण आयन नकिट-मृत्यु अनुभव का क्षेत्र है। वे विशिष्ट घटनाओं के दस्तावेजीकरण और शोध के लिए सख्त मानकों का उपयोग करते हुए वर्जीनिया विश्वविद्यालय जैसे स्थानों पर शीर्ष वैज्ञानिक रहे हैं। वे भौतिक विज्ञान के सभी ज्ञात कानूनों के अनुसार तकनीकी रूप से बेहोशी की स्थिति में, या दिल का दौरा या दुर्घटना के कारण कोमा में रोगियों के साथ सैकड़ों परीक्षण मामलों में प्रदर्शनकारी निर्णायक निष्कर्ष निकालने में सक्षम रहे हैं। होश में आने के बाद मरीजों ने विस्तार से बताया कि उन्हें पुनर्जीवित करने के लिए क्या प्रक्रियाएं की गई थीं। वे खुद को अपने शरीर से बाहर तैरते हुए, ऊपर कमरे में, नीचे देख रहे हैं और उन चिकित्सा प्रक्रियाओं को देख रहे हैं जो डॉक्टर उन पर कर रहे थे। इस बात की कोई संभावना नहीं थी कि वे ऐसा सपना देख सकते थे जैसा कि बाद के परीक्षणों ने दिखाया है। इससे पता चलता है कि मस्तिष्क और दिमाग के बीच एक अंतर है, और यह कि दिमाग या चेतना काम करना जारी रख सकती है, भले ही मस्तिष्क बिगड़ा हुआ हो और शायद ही काम कर रहा हो, जैसा कि बेहोश अवस्था में होता है।

नकिट-मृत्यु के अनुभव में हमारे पास यह वर्णन है कि जब वे पुनर्जीवित हुए तो व्यक्तियों के साथ क्या हुआ, लेकिन क्या होगा यदि वे अपने शरीर में फिर से प्रवेश नहीं करते? क्या होगा अगर मरीजों को पुनर्जीवित नहीं किया जा सकता है? अगर वे मर गए होते तो कहां जाते? या मौत बस सब कुछ का अंत है? जब कोई मरता है, तो रिश्तेदार रो सकते हैं और कह सकते हैं, "अरे, वह चला गया, वह हमें छोड़कर चला गया।" लेकिन वह क्या चला गया है? वह वहीं पड़ा है, या कम से कम शरीर है। तो, अगर वह चला गया, तो यह वह हिस्सा है जिसे आपने देखा नहीं है जो चला गया है। लेकिन यह क्या है?

जैसा कि हमने पिछले कई पन्नों में दिखाया है, दार्शनिकों और वैज्ञानिकों ने इस पर सवाल उठाए हैं और किसी अंतिम निष्कर्ष पर नहीं पहुंचे हैं। लेकिन वैदिक साहित्य स्वयं का विस्तृत विवरण देता है। छांदोग्य उपनिषद (6.10.3) यह समझाना शुरू करता है कि जो कुछ भी मौजूद है उसमें सूक्ष्म सार स्वयं है। यह सत्य है और तू ही है।

ट्वेल में छांदोग्य उपनिषद के पाँचवें और तेरहवें खंड में, यह आगे के उदाहरण देता है जिसमें यह कहा गया है कि एक ऊँचे पेड़ का अपना सार है, स्वयं, मूल रूप से उस छोटे से बीज में जिसमें वह बढ़ता है। फिर भी, एक बीज को तोड़ने से इतने बड़े पौधे के रूप में विकसित होने की कोई क्षमता प्रकट नहीं होगी। लेकिन शक्ति है। इसी प्रकार नमक लेकर पानी में मिलाने से नमक अदृश्य हो जाता है; फिर भी, पानी को चखकर हम जान सकते हैं कि नमक है। इसी तरह, भौतिक शरीर में, आत्मा मौजूद है, हालांकि हम इसे प्रत्यक्ष रूप से अनुभव नहीं करते हैं। हालाँकि, भगवद-गीता (13.34) बताती है: "हे भरत के पुत्र, जैसे कि अकेले सूर्य इस पूरे ब्रह्मांड को रोशन करता है, वैसे ही जीव, शरीर के भीतर एक, चेतना द्वारा पूरे शरीर को रोशन करता है।" इसलिए जिस प्रकार जल में मिले हुए नमक को हम चेतना के लक्षण को पहचाने बिना नहीं देख सकते।

एक छोटा सा प्रयोग करके चेतना को आसानी से पहचाना जा सकता है, अपने शरीर के हिस्से को चुभोओ और आप दर्द भर देंगे। यह न केवल मनुष्यों में बल्कि खाने वालों, कुत्तों या अन्य जानवरों में भी चेतना का लक्षण है। जीवन की किसी भी प्रकार की प्रजाति में, दो प्रकार के शरीर होते हैं; शरीर जो जीवित है, और शरीर जो मर चुका है और बिगड़ रहा है। जीवात्मा आत्मा की चेतना से व्याप्त और प्रकाशित है। मुंडक उपनिषद (3.1.9) कहता है: "आत्मा आकार में परमाणु है और इसे पूर्ण बुद्धि द्वारा देखा जा सकता है। यह परमाणु आत्मा पाँच प्रकार की वायु (प्राण, अपान, व्यान, समान और उदान) में तैर रही है, हृदय के भीतर स्थित है, और देहधारी जीवों के पूरे शरीर में अपना प्रभाव फैलाती है। जब आत्मा को पाँच प्रकार की भौतिक वायु के दूषित होने से शुद्ध किया जाता है, तो इसका आध्यात्मिक प्रभाव प्रदर्शित होता है।

इस प्रकार, स्व शरीर के भीतर प्रेरक कारक है और जब यह निकल जाता है, तो शरीर टूट जाता है और धीरे-धीरे विघटित हो जाता है। इसलिए, बृहदारण्यक उपनिषद (2.4.3-5) बताता है कि जो भी हमें प्रिय है, चाहे वह हमारी पत्नियाँ हों, पति हों, पुत्र हों, पुत्रियाँ हों, शिक्षक हों, अभिभावक हों, आदि हों, वे हमें केवल उनकी उपस्थिति के कारण प्रिय हैं।

शरीर के भीतर आत्मा, जो वास्तव में हमें प्ररिय हौ एक बार जब स्व शरीर को छोड़ देता है, तो शरीर हमारे लिए अनाकर्षक हो जाता है क्योंकि यह तेजी से ठंडा, कठोर हो जाता है और सडऩे लगता हौ इसलिए शरीर हमारी वास्तवकि पहचान नहीं है, बल्कि हम भीतर स्वयं हौं

आत्मा शाश्वत है

छ्रांदोग्य उपनिषद (6.11.3) में यह भी कहा गया है कि यद्यपि शरीर मुरझा जाता है और मर जाता है जब स्वयं इसे छोड़ देता है, जीवति स्वयं मरता नहीं हौ बाइबल यह भी समझाती है: "हम तो देखी हुई वस्तुओं को नहीं परन्तु अनदेखी वस्तुओं को देखते रहते हैं; उन चीजों के लिए जो लौककि दिखाई देती हैं; परन्तु जो वस्तुएं दिखाई नहीं देती वे सदा बनी रहती हौं" (2 कुरिन्थियों 4:18)

श्रीमद-भागवतम (7.2.22) में आगे की प्रबद्धता दी गई है: "आत्मा, जीव की कोई मृत्यु नहीं है, क्योंकि वह शाश्वत और अक्षय हौ भौतकि कल्मष से मुक्त होने के कारण, वह भौतकि या आध्यात्मकि दुनिया में कहीं भी जा सकता हौ वह पूरी तरह से जागरूक है और भौतकि शरीर से पूरी तरह से अलग है, लेकनि अपनी थोड़ी सी स्वतंत्रता के दुरुपयोग से गुमराह होने के कारण, वह भौतकि ऊर्जा द्वारा बनाए गए सूक्ष्म और स्थूल शरीर को स्वीकार करने के लिए बाध्य है और इस प्रकार तथाकथति भौतकि सुख और संकट के अधीन हौ . इसलिए, कसिी को आत्मा के शरीर से नकिल जाने पर शोक नहीं करना चाहिए।"

स्वयं की शाश्वत प्रकृति को श्री कृष्ण द्वारा भगवद-गीता में भी समझाया गया है: "कभी भी ऐसा समय नहीं था जब मैं अस्तत्वि में नहीं था, न ही तुम, न ही ये सभी राजा; न ही भवष्यि में हममें से कोई भी नहीं रहेगा। जसि प्रकार दहेधारी आत्मा नरिन्तर इस शरीर में, लडक़पन से युवावस्था और वृद्धावस्था में गुजरती है, उसी प्रकार मृत्यु के समय आत्मा दूसरे शरीर में जाती हौ आत्मसाक्षातकारी आत्मा इस प्रकार के परविर्तन से मोहग्रस्त नहीं होती।" (भ.गी.2.12-13)

"जान लो कि जो पूरे शरीर में व्याप्त है वह अवनिाशी हौ अवनिाशी आत्मा को कोई नष्ट नहीं कर सकता। केवल अवनिाशी, अथाह और

शाश्वत जीव का भौतिक शरीर ही विनाश के अधीन है (भ.गी.2.17-18)... आत्मा के लिए न तो कभी जन्म होता है और न ही मृत्यु। न ही एक बार होने के बाद वह कभी नहीं रहता। वह अजन्मा, नित्य, सदा-विद्यमान, अविनाशी और आदिम है शरीर के मार जाने पर वह मारा नहीं जाता। (भ.गी.2.20)... जैसे मनुष्य पुराने वस्त्रों को त्याग कर नए वस्त्र धारण करता है, उसी प्रकार आत्मा पुराने और अनुपयोगी शरीरों को त्याग कर नए भौतिक शरीरों को ग्रहण करती है। (भ. गी. 2.23)

निश्चित रूप से यह ज्ञान किसी को भी उस चिंता से छुटकारा दिला सकता है जो यह सोचने से आती है कि मृत्यु पर हमारा अस्तित्व समाप्त हो गया है।

आत्मिक रूप से, हम मरते नहीं हैं; फिर भी, शरीर का उपयोग तब तक किया जाता है जब तक कि वह जारी रखने के लिए फिट नहीं हो जाता। उस समय ऐसा लग सकता है कि हम मर रहे हैं, लेकिन ऐसा नहीं है। आत्मा अपने प्रारब्ध के अनुसार दूसरे शरीर में अपनी यात्रा करती रहती है और अगर किसी ने ईमानदारी से अभ्यास किया है और एक वास्तविक आध्यात्मिक मार्ग को सिद्ध किया है, तो उसका अगला शरीर भौतिक नहीं होगा, बल्कि पूरी तरह से आध्यात्मिक हो सकता है।

आत्मा की अविनाशीता के आगे के विवरण को इस तरह से समझाया गया है जिससे पता चलता है कि यह सभी भौतिक तत्वों के प्रभाव से कैसे परे है।

"आत्मा सी n वह कभी किसी शस्त्र से टुकड़े-टुकड़े न हो, न आग से जलाया जाए, न वायु से सुखाया जाए। यह व्यक्तिगत आत्मा अटूट और अघुलनशील है, और इसे न तो जलाया जा सकता है और न ही सुखाया जा सकता है। वह नित्य, सर्वव्यापी, अपरिवर्तनीय, अचल और नित्य एक ही है। कहा जाता है कि आत्मा अदृश्य, अपरिवर्तनीय और अपरिवर्तनीय है। यह जानकर, तुम्हें शरीर के लिए शोक नहीं करना चाहिए" (भ. गी. 2.23.25)

"कोई आत्मा को अद्भुत देखता है, कोई उसे अद्भुत बताता है और कोई उसे अद्भुत सुनता है, जबकि कोई उसके बारे में सुनकर भी उसे बिल्कुल नहीं समझ सकता। हे भरत के वंशज, वह जो शरीर में रहता है वह शाश्वत

है और कभी भी मारा नहीं जा सकता। इसलिए तुम्हें किसी प्राणी के लिए शोक करने की आवश्यकता नहीं है" (भ. गी. 2.29-30)

हम ध्यान दें कि जब यह कहता है कि किसी भी प्राणी के लिए शोक नहीं करना चाहिए, तो इसका मतलब यह नहीं है कि अगर हम किसी प्राणी या पीड़ित व्यक्ति को देखते हैं कि हम स्थिति के प्रति उदासीन या कठोर बने रहते हैं। जब हम किसी को पीड़ित देखते हैं, तो हमें करुणा महसूस करनी चाहिए। करुणा एक ऐसा गुण है जो किसी को कोमल हृदय और दूसरों की भलाई के लिए चिंतित महसूस कराएगा। ऐसा गुण उसके लिए आवश्यक है जो भीतर के व्यक्ति में फिट होने की कोशिश कर रहा है। वास्तविकता को देखने का अर्थ है सभी के आध्यात्मिक स्वरूप को पहचानना।

आत्मा का वैदिक विवरण

श्रीमद-भागवतम (11.28.35) बताता है कि स्वयं स्वयं-प्रकाशमान है, जन्म और मृत्यु से परे है, और समय या स्थान से असीमित है और इसलिए, सभी परिवर्तनों से परे है। भागवतम (11.22.50) यह भी बताता है कि जैसे कोई एक पेड़ के जन्म और मृत्यु का गवाह होता है और उससे अलग होता है, उसी तरह जन्म, मृत्यु और शरीर की विभिन्न गतिविधियों का गवाह उससे अलग होता है। भगवद गीता में भी कहा गया है: "जो यह देख सकता है कि सभी गतिविधियाँ शरीर द्वारा की जाती हैं, जो भौतिक प्रकृति से निर्मित है, और देखता है कि स्वयं कुछ भी नहीं करता है, वास्तव में देखता है। जब एक समझदार व्यक्ति अलग-अलग पहचानों को देखने के लिए तैयार होता है, जो विभिन्न भौतिक शरीरों के कारण होते हैं, तो वह ब्रह्म अवधारणा को प्राप्त करता है। इस प्रकार, वह देखता है कि प्राणियों का विस्तार हर जगह है। अनंत काल की दृष्टि वाले लोग देख सकते हैं कि आत्मा पारलौकिक, शाश्वत और प्रकृति के गुणों से परे है। भौतिक शरीर के संपर्क के बावजूद । हे अर्जुन, आत्मा न तो कुछ करती है और न ही फंसती है। आकाश अपनी सूक्ष्म प्रकृति के कारण सर्वव्यापक होते हुए भी किसी वस्तु से मिश्रित नहीं होता। इसी प्रकार ब्रह्म दृष्टि में स्थित जीवात्मा उस शरीर में स्थित होते हुए भी शरीर को नहीं मिलाता। (भ. गी. 13.30-33)

छांदोग्य उपनषिद (6.3.3) के अनुसार, यद्यपि आत्मा शरीर में स्थति है, यह बहुत छोटा है और हृदय में विराजमान है। हम इसे देख सकते हैं क्योंकि शरीर के भीतर की सारी ऊर्जा हृदय से फैलती है। अगर दिल काम करना बंद कर दे तो पूरा शरीर ढह जाता है। लेकनि हृदय केवल एक आसन है, जिसका अर्थ है कि आसन को बदला जा सकता है जैसा कि हम हृदय प्रत्यारोपण संचालन से या स्वयं का ज्ञान प्राप्त करने के लिए यांत्रिक के उपयोग से भी देख सकते हैं। इसलिए, हमें करुणा महसूस करनी चाहिए और यदि हम कर सकते हैं तो दूसरों की समस्याओं को हल करने में मदद करें। लेकनि करुणा महसूस करने का मतलब केवल भूखे लोगों को कुछ खाने को देना नहीं है। बेशक, यह किया जाना चाहिए अगर हम ऐसा करने में सक्षम हैं, लेकनि वास्तवकि करुणा का अर्थ है उनकी वास्तवकि स्थति और आध्यात्मकि पहचान को समझने में उनकी मदद करना।

उदाहरण के लिए, जैसा कि हमने समझाया है, शरीर घटता है और मर जाता है, लेकनि आत्मा मरती नहीं है: यह सिर्फ शरीर बदलती है। इसलिए शरीर एक कमीज या कोट की तरह है जिसे हम कुछ समय के लिए पहनते हैं और जब वह पुराना हो जाता है तो हम उसे बदल कर नया ले लेते हैं। तो, अगर हमें किसी ऐसे व्यक्ति को देखना चाहिए जो पीडति है और भौतकि प्रकृति से संघर्ष कर रहा है, जैसे कि एक डूबता हुआ आदमी, तो उसके पास जाने और केवल उसकी कमीज या कोट को बचाने का क्या फायदा है? हम यह सोचकर किनारे पर वापस तैरेंगे, "मैंने उसे बचा लिया है," और पाते हैं कि हम जो कुछ भी वापस लाए हैं, वह उसकी शर्ट है, जबकि वास्तवकि व्यक्ति अभी भी भौतकि ऊर्जा के सागर में पीडति है। हमें कमीज या भौतकि शरीर के भीतर व्यक्ति या आत्मा का भी ध्यान रखना चाहिए। जब तक किसी के पास एक भौतकि शरीर है, चाहे इस जीवन में या इसके बाद कितने ही जन्मों में, जन्म, रोग, बुढ़ापा और मृत्यु जैसी कई अपरिहार्य समस्याएं होंगी। इसलिए, वैदकि साहित्य, जैसे छांदोग्य उपनषिद (8.1.1) में उल्लेख किया गया है कि स्वयं के भीतर का ज्ञान वह है जिसे सभी को खोजना और समझना चाहिए। अपनी आध्यात्मकि पहचान को समझने से जीवन की सभी समस्याओं का समाधान हो जाता है,

जैसा कि हम इस अध्याय में आगे स्पष्ट करेंगे।

जितना अधिक हम अपनी आध्यात्मिक पहचान को महसूस करेंगे, उतना ही अधिक हम देखेंगे कि हम इन अस्थायी भौतिक शरीरों से परे हैं, और यह कि हमारी पहचान केवल एक सफेद शरीर, या काला, या पीला, या मोटा, पतला, बुद्धिमान, गूंगा, बूढ़ा होना नहीं है, युवा, मजबूत, कमजोर, अंधा, आदि। वास्तविक अंधापन का अर्थ अस्थायी और सतही शारीरिक स्थितियों और हृदय के माध्यम से देखने में सक्षम नहीं होना है। लेकिन इतनी वैज्ञानिक प्रगति के बाद भी अगर आत्मा शरीर छोड़ दे तो एक यांत्रिक हृदय भी लंबे समय तक शरीर को क्रियाशील नहीं रख पाएगा।

श्वेताश्वतर उपनिषद (5.9) में आत्मा के आकार का वर्णन किया गया है: "जब ऊपरी एक बाल के बिंदु को एक सौ भागों में विभाजित किया जाता है और फिर ऐसे प्रत्येक भाग को एक सौ भागों में विभाजित किया जाता है, ऐसा प्रत्येक भाग आत्मा के आयाम का माप है।"

भागवतम में यह भी कहा गया है: "आध्यात्मिक परमाणुओं के असंख्य कण हैं, जिन्हें बालों के ऊपरी हिस्से के दस-हजारवें हिस्से के रूप में मापा जाता है।" तो, स्पष्ट रूप से, यदि आप एक बाल का सटीक सिरा लेते हैं, जो आम तौर पर एक इंच के तीन हजारवें हिस्से के व्यास को मापता है, और इसे दस हजार टुकड़ों में काटता है, तो ऐसा एक टुकड़ा व्यावहारिक रूप से अदृश्य, परमाणु आकार का होगा। इसलिए, यदि भौतिक पदार्थों के परमाणुओं का पता लगाने के लिए विशिष्ट उपकरण की आवश्यकता होती है, तो इसमें कोई आश्चर्य नहीं है कि वैज्ञानिक उपकरण उन परमाणु कणों का पता नहीं लगा सकते हैं जो आध्यात्मिक हैं। भले ही वैज्ञानिक प्रलेखित प्रमाण चाहते हैं कि आत्मा जैसी कोई चीज है, वैदिक साहित्य का अध्ययन करके, हम सीखते हैं कि आत्मा को सामान्य वैज्ञानिक उपकरणों द्वारा नहीं देखा जा सकता है। बेशक, जैसा कि हमने स्थापित किया है, आत्मा को देखने के अन्य तरीके हैं, विशिष्ट रूप से योग विज्ञान और वैदिक विज्ञान के अध्ययन के माध्यम से। हमारा सुझाव है कि ये वैज्ञानिक वेदों का अध्ययन यह जानने के लिए करें कि उनकी सीमित इन्द्रिय धारणा से परे क्या है।

तथ्य यह है कि ज्यादातर लोगों ने परमाणु जैसे प्रोटॉन और न्यूट्रॉन आदि नहीं देखे हैं, जनिके बारे में वैज्ञानिक बात करते हों वे केवल वैज्ञानिकों की बात मान सकते हैं कि ऐसी चीजें मौजूद हैं इसी प्रकार बहुत से लोगों ने आत्मा को प्रत्यक्ष रूप से नहीं देखा है वे केवल उन्हीं की बात मान सकते हैं जो जानने वाले हैं लेकिन, जैसा कि पहले बताया गया है, कोई भी उस चेतना को पहचान सकता है जो शरीर में व्याप्त है, जो आत्मा का लक्षण है यह मुश्किल नहीं है यदि आप किसी जीव को, चाहे वह व्यक्ति, बिल्ली, कुत्ता, आदि हों, चिकोटी काटते हैं या कुछ पीडा़ पहुँचाते हैं, या किसी जंगली जानवर जैसे पक्षी या गिलहरी के पास जाते हैं, तो वह दूर जाने की कोशिश करेगा। यह कोई सहज प्रतिविर्त नहीं है, बल्कि यह चेतना के कारण है और यह वैदिक विज्ञान के अनुसार आत्मा के अस्तित्व का प्रत्यक्ष प्रमाण है, जिससे चेतना शरीर के माध्यम से फैलती है

वेदों के अनुसार शरीर की तुलना एक रथ से की गई है जिसमें स्वयं सवार है "ज्ञान में उन्नत अध्यात्मवादी भगवान के आदेश से बने शरीर की तुलना एक रथ से करते हैं इन्द्रियाँ घोडो़ं के समान हैं; मन, इन्द्रियों का स्वामी, लगाम के समान है; इन्द्रियों के विषिय ही गन्तव्य हैं; बुद्धि सारथी है; और चेतना, जो पूरे शरीर में फैलती है, इस भौतिक संसार में बंधन का कारण है (भाग.7.15.41)

इस उदाहरण में, इन्द्रियाँ घोडो़ं की तरह हैं जो हमेशा मन को उस वस्तु की ओर खींचती हैं जिससे वे आकर्षित होती हैं मन सदैव अशांत, अशांत, हठी और अत्यंत बलवान होता है योग के अभ्यास से ही मन को नियित्रति किया जा सकता है अन्यथा, मन हमेशा इंद्रियों को संतुष्ट करने के लिए योजना बनाने के लिए बुद्धि को समझाने की कोशिश कर रहा है इस प्रकार, बुद्धि, जिसे रथ चालक के रूप में संदर्भित किया जाता है, आज यहाँ और वहाँ ले जाएगा, इस आशा में कि वे देखने, स्वाद, महसूस करने, सुनने और सूंघने जैसी अच्छी वस्तुओं के गंतव्य तक पहुँच जाएँ इस बीच, शरीर के भीतर स्वयं सवारी कर रहा है और इन सभी गतिविधियों को देख रहा है

कटब उपनषिद (1.3.3-12) में, जो एक ही उदाहरण देता है, वहाँ और वस्तिार है जहाँ यह कहा गया है कि जिसिके पास कोई समझ नहीं है और जिसिका मन (लगाम) कभी भी दढ़ृता से नहीं होता है, उसकी इंद्रयिाँ (घोड) असहनीय होती हैं, एक सारथी के शातरि घोडों की तरह। परन्त् जिसिके पास समझ है और जिसिका मन दढ़ृ. है, उसकी इन्द्रयिाँ सारथी के अच्छे घोडों की तरह वश में हों जिसिके पास कोई समझ नहीं है वह प्नर्जन्म के दौर में प्रवेश करता है; जबकि; जिसिके पास समझ है, जो मननशील और पवत्रि है, वह उस स्थान पर पहुँच जाता है जहाँ से उसका फरि से जन्म नहीं होता। वह अपनी यात्रा के अंत तक पहुँचता है, जो आध्यात्मकि वातावरण में श्री वष्णिु का सर्वोच्च स्थान हो।

कतबा उपनषिद यह भी बताता है कि शरीर के भीतर, इंद्रयिों और इंद्रयिों की वस्तुओं से उच्चतर, मन मौजूद हो। मन से अधकि सूक्ष्म बद्धुि है, और बद्धुि से उच्च और सूक्ष्म आत्मा हो। वह आत्मा सभी प्राणयिों में छिपी हुई है और प्रकाशति नहीं होती, बल्कि सूक्ष्म दष्टृटा अपनी तीक्ष्ण बद्धुि से देखते हों।

इससे हम समझ सकते हैं कि स्थूल भौतकि शरीर के भीतर, वभिन्नि भौतकि तत्वों, जैसे पृथ्वी, वायु, जल, आदि की तुलना में मन, बद्धुि और अहंकार के सूक्ष्म सूक्ष्म तत्वों से बना सूक्ष्म शरीर भी हो। मानसकि गतवविधियिाँ सूक्ष्म शरीर के भीतर होती हैं, और जब बेलगाम इंद्रयिाँ और मन कसिी व्यक्ति के लक्ष्यों और इच्छाओं के नयिंत्रक होते हैं, तो मन की मांगों को पूरा करने में, या मनोवशिलेषण को शांत करने की आशा के साथ बहुत समय व्यतीत कयिा जा सकता हो। मन और उसके भीतर मौजूद समस्याओं का पता लगाना। इस प्रकार, बहुत से लोग महसूस करते हैं कि मन की संतुष्टटि प्राप्त करना ही जीवन का लक्ष्य है, और फरि वभिन्नि और कभी-कभी महंगे कार्यक्रमों में भाग लेते हैं जो इसे पूरा करने का वादा करते हों।

मन का शांत होना एक भरोसा हो सकता है ऐसे कसिी भी व्यक्ति के लिए एफई जिसि इस तरह की मानसकि समस्याएं हैं और वह आराम करने या बेहतर नींद लेने या एक खुशहाल और स्वस्थ जीवन जीने का

तरीका ढूंढ रहा हूँ यह इन दिनों लोगों के लिए अधिक महत्वपूर्ण होता जा रहा है, विशिष्ट रूप से पश्चिमी सभ्यता में जहां वे मनश्चिकित्सीय उपचार का उपयोग कर सकते हैं, या मन पर नियंत्रण या सम्मोहन में विशिष्ट पाठ्यक्रम ले सकते हैं, या अपने मन पर अधिक नियंत्रण प्राप्त करने या अपने परिवर्तन को बदलने के लिए विशिष्ट अचेतन-संदेश टेप का उपयोग कर सकते हैं। रवैया और उनका जीवन। लेकिन यह भी योग के उद्देश्यों में से एक है, जिसका अभ्यास हजारों वर्षों से बहुत प्रभावी ढंग से किया जाता रहा है। इसलिए, भगवद-गीता इस बात पर जोर देती है कि व्यक्ति को निम्न आत्म को उच्च आत्म द्वारा नियंत्रित करना चाहिए। मन हमेशा इंद्रिय संतुष्टि की गतिविधियों में संलग्न होना चाहता है और इसलिए, जीवन के लक्ष्य के ज्ञान को विकसित करने के बाद बुद्धि द्वारा निर्देशित किया जाना चाहिए। इन्द्रियविषयों में लीन मन भौतिक गतिविधियों के बंधन का कारण है, और इन्द्रियविषयों से विरक्त मन मुक्ति का कारण है।

''व्यक्ति को अपने मन से खुद को ऊपर उठाना चाहिए, खुद को नीचा नहीं दिखाना चाहिए। मध्य बद्धजीव का मित्र है और शत्रु भी। जिसने मन को जीत लिया है, उसके लिए मन सबसे अच्छा मित्र है; लेकिन जो ऐसा करने में विफल रहा है, उसके लिए उसका दिमाग ही सबसे बड़ा दुश्मन हो सकता है (भ. गी. 6.5-6)।

भगवद-गीता में, श्रीकृष्ण भी सलाह देते हैं: "जिस प्रकार वायु रहित स्थान में दीपक डगमगाता नहीं है, उसी प्रकार पारलौकिकवादी, जिसका मन नियंत्रित होता है, पारलौकिक आत्मा पर अपने ध्यान में हमेशा स्थिर रहता है। मन अपनी चंचलता और चंचलता के कारण जहाँ-जहाँ भटके, वहाँ-वहाँ से हटाकर आत्मा के वश में कर लेना चाहिए। जिसका मन निरंकुश है, उसके लिए आत्म-साक्षात्कार कठिन काम है परन्तु जिसका मन वश में है और जो उचित साधनों से प्रयत्न करता है, उसकी सफलता सुनिश्चित है। यह मेरी राय है (भ. 6.19,26,36)

हालाँकि, इस आधुनिक समय में, हम देखते हैं कि आमतौर पर यह सलाह दी जाती है कि आप जो भी करना चाहते हैं, अगर इससे किसी को ठेस नहीं

पहुँचती है, तो ठीक है। अच्छा लगता है, तो इसे करो। लेकिन वैदिक ग्रंथों में हम देखते हैं कि मन को जितना हो सके उतना स्वतंत्र होने देने का यह आधुनिक दर्शन आज समाज में भ्रम की आग में घी डालने का काम करता है। भगवद गीता से सलाह लेकर हम निश्चित रूप से मानसिक समस्याओं को हल करना सीख सकते हैं। मन की ये गडबडी अभी भी बहुत सतही स्तर पर है क्योंकि वास्तविक आत्म मन और बुद्धि से ऊपर है जो मन को नियंत्रित कर सकता है। इसलिए, हमें स्वयं को समझने के लिए मन और बुद्धि के सूक्ष्म तत्वों से ऊपर उठना होगा:

"रूप की इस स्थूल अवधारणा से परे [शरीर] रूप की एक और सूक्ष्म अवधारणा है [सूक्ष्म शरीर या मन, बुद्धि, और मिथ्या अहंकार] जो औपचारिक आकार के बिना है और अनदेखी, अनसुनी और अव्यक्त है। इस सूक्ष्मता से परे जीव का अपना रूप है, अन्यथा वह बार-बार जन्म न ले पाता। जब भी कोई व्यक्ति आत्म-साक्षात्कार द्वारा यह अनुभव करता है कि स्थूल और सूक्ष्म दोनों शरीरो का शुद्ध आत्मा से कोई लेना-देना नहीं है, उस समय वह स्वयं के साथ-साथ भगवान को भी देखता है। (भ.गी.1.3.32-33)

चूँकि हम स्थूल और सूक्ष्म शरीरो से अलग हैं, हम भौतिक शरीर के साथ इतनी दृढ़ता से तादात्म्य क्यों रखते हैं? इसे इस प्रकार समझाया गया है: "यद्यपि भौतिक शरीर स्वयं से भिन्न है, भौतिक संगति की अज्ञानता के कारण व्यक्ति स्वयं को श्रेष्ठ और हीन शारीरिक स्थितियो के साथ पहचानता है। कभी-कभी एक भाग्यशाली व्यक्ति इस तरह की मानसिक मनगढ़ंत कहानी को त्यागने में सक्षम होता है। (भाग. I. 22.48)

"झूठा अहंकार भ्रामक भौतिक अस्तित्व को आकार देता है और इस प्रकार भौतिक सुख और संकट का अनुभव करता है। हालाँकि, आत्मा भौतिक प्रकृति से परे है; वह वास्तव में किसी भी स्थान पर, किसी भी परिस्थिति में या किसी व्यक्ति की एजेंसी से भौतिक सुख और संकट से प्रभावित नहीं हो सकता है। जो व्यक्ति इसे समझता है उसे भौतिक सृष्टि से डरने की कोई बात नहीं है" (भाग. I. 23.56)

"अपनी मानसकि उलझन के अलावा कोई अन्य शक्ति आत्मा को सुख और संकट का अनुभव नहीं कराती हौ मत्रिों, तटस्थ दलों और शत्रुओं के बारे में उनकी धारणा और इस धारणा के इर्द-गर्दि नर्मिति संपूर्ण भौतकि जीवन केवल अज्ञानता से नर्मिति हौ (भाग. I. 23.59)

इन श्लोकों में यह स्पष्ट रूप से समझाया गया है कि केवल मथ्यिा अहंकार के कारण ही हम सोचते हैं कि हम भौतकि शरीर हैं, और ऐसी धारणा से हम तुरंत वभिन्नि भौतकि इच्छाओं का अनुभव करते हैं जो सुख या दुख का कारण बनती हौ हालाँकि, वास्तवकि अहंकार की भावना है, जैसे, "मैं काला हूँ" "मैं सफेद हूँ" या सोचता है कि वे मोटे, पतले, छोटे, लम्बे, अमरेकिी, यूरोपीय, हंदिू, मुस्लमि, कैथोलकि, प्रोटस्ेट्टें हौ आदि, यह सब मथ्यिा अहंकार है। यह हमारी वास्तवकि पहचान के लिए सतही है, लेकनि यह अज्ञान दुनिया भर के लोगों, समुदायों, पडो़सयिों या राष्ट्रों के बीच बाधाओं, झगडो़ं और गलतफहमयिों का कारण हौ हालाँकि, जब मथ्यिा अहंकार, माया या भ्रम का एक उत्पाद, जो स्वयं की वास्तवकि प्रकृति को ढंकता है, स्वयं के ज्ञान में जांच के खंजर से काट दयिा जाता हैं, जो पूर्ण आत्मा है फरि आनंदति होता हौ इस स्थतिि को स्थायी वघिटन कहा जाता हौ केवल इसी स्थतिि में दुनिया के लोग वास्तव में शांति का अनुभव करेंगे, या तो व्यक्तगित रूप से या वश्विव्यापी आधार पर।

श्रीमद-भागवतम् (पाँचवाँ सर्ग, अध्याय दस) में स्वयं को शरीर से अलग करने के बारे में वस्तिार से बतानेवाली एक कहानी है, जसिमें जड़ भरत नाम के एक आत्म-साक्षात्कारी भक्त को राजा रहूगण की पालकी ले जाने में मदद करने के लिए मजबूर कयिा जाता हौ पास यात्रा कर रहा हौ राजा को एक अतरिक्ति वाहक की आवश्यकता होती है और जब राजा के आदमी को जड़ भरत मलि जाता है, तो वे उसे मदद करने के लिए मजबूर करते हौ

पालकी को बहुत आसानी से नहीं ले जाया जा रहा है और राजा, जड़ भरत होने का कारण खोज रहा है, उसे बहुत गंभीर रूप से दंडति करता हौ राजा बहुत क्रोधति होकर कहता है, "धूर्त, यह क्या कर रहा है? क्या आप अपने शरीर के भीतर जीवन के बावजूद मर चुके हैं? क्या तुम नहीं जानते

कि मैं तुम्हारा स्वामी हूँ तुम मेरी अवहेलना कर रहे हो और मेरे आदेश का पालन नहीं कर रहे हो। इस अनाज्ञाकारिता के लिए अब मैं तुम्हें दण्ड दूँगा और तुम्हारा उचित उपचार करूँगा ताकि तुम अपने होश में आओ और सही काम करो।

राजा रहूगण अपने आप को राजा मानते हुए शारीरिक अवधारणा में हैं और भौतिक प्रकृति के रजोगुण और अज्ञानता से प्रभावित हों पागलपन के कारण, वह जड़ भरत को अकारण और विरोधाभासी शब्दों से डांटता हों जड़ भरत सर्वोच्च भक्त हों यद्यपि स्वयं को बहुत विद्वान मानते हुए, राजा भक्ति-योग में स्थित एक उन्नत भक्त की स्थिति के बारे में नहीं जानता, न ही वह उसकी विशेषताओं को जानता हों जड़ भरत सर्वोच्च भगवान का निवास स्थान हैं; वह हमेशा अपने हृदय के भीतर प्रभु के रूप को धारण करता हों वह सभी जीवों के प्रति मित्र हैं, और किसी भी शारीरिक गर्भाधान का मनोरंजन नहीं करते हों इसलिए वह मुस्कुराता हैं और निम्नलिखित शब्द बोलता हैं:

"मेरे प्रिय राजा और नायक, आपने जो कुछ भी व्यंग्यात्मक रूप से कहा हैं वह निश्चित रूप से सत्य हों दरअसल, ये केवल ताड़ना के शब्द नहीं हैं, क्योंकि शरीर वाहक हों शरीर द्वारा उठाया गया भार मेरा नहीं हैं, क्योंकि मैं आत्मा हूँ आपकी बातों में कोई विरोधाभास नहीं हैं क्योंकि मैं शरीर से अलग हूं मैं पालकी का वाहक नहीं हूं शरीर वाहक हों निश्चित ही, जैसा कि आपने संकेत किया हैं, मैंने पालकी उठाने का श्रम नहीं किया हैं, क्योंकि मैं शरीर से अलग हूँ तुमने कहा हैं कि मैं हृष्ट-पुष्ट और बलवान नहीं हूँ और ये शब्द उस व्यक्ति को लाभ पहुँचा रहे हैं जो शरीर और आत्मा के बीच के भेद को नहीं जानता। शरीर मोटा या पतला हो सकता हैं, लेकिन कोई विद्वान व्यक्ति आत्मा की ऐसी बातें नहीं कहेगा। जहां तक आत्मा का संबंध हैं, मैं न तो मोटा हूं और न ही पतला; इसलिए, जब आप कहते हैं कि मैं बहुत मोटा नहीं हूँ तो आप सही हों साथ ही, अगर इस यात्रा का उद्देश्य और वहां जाने वाला रास्ता मेरा होता, तो मेरे लिए बहुत परेशानी होती, लेकिन चूंकि वे मुझस नहीं बल्कि मेरे शरीर से संबंधित हैं, इसलिए कोई परेशानी नहीं हों

"मोटापन, पतलापन, शारीरिक और मानसिक कष्ट, प्यास, भूख, भय, असहमति, भौतिक सुख की इच्छा, बुढ़ापा, नींद, भौतिक वस्तुओं के प्रति आसक्ति, क्रोध, विलाप, भ्रम और स्वयं के साथ शरीर की पहचान सभी के रूपांतर हैं आत्मा का भौतिक आवरण। भौतिक शारीरिक धारणाओं में लीन एक व्यक्ति। नतीजतन, मैं न तो मोटा हूं और न ही पतला और न ही कुछ और जिसका आपने उल्लेख किया हो।

"मेरे प्रिय राजा, आपने अनावश्यक रूप से मुझ पर जीवित होते हुए भी मृत होने का आरोप लगाया हो। इस संबंध में मैं केवल इतना ही कह सकता हूं कि हर जगह यही स्थिति है क्योंकि हर भौतिक वस्तु का आदि और अंत होता है। जहाँ तक आपका यह विचार है कि आप राजा और स्वामी हैं और इस प्रकार मुझे आदेश देने का प्रयास कर रहे हैं, यह भी गलत है क्योंकि ये पद अस्थायी हैं। आज आप राजा हैं और मैं आपका सेवक, लेकिन कल स्थिति बदल सकती है, और आप मेरे सेवक हो सकते हैं और मैं आपका स्वामी। ये प्रोवडिंस द्वारा बनाई गई अस्थायी परिस्थितियां हैं। प्रत्येक व्यक्ति को इन पदों पर भौतिक प्रकृति के नियमों द्वारा विविश किया जा रहा है; इसलिए, वास्तव में न तो कोई स्वामी है और न ही कोई सेवक है।"

View From Students

1. I was introduced to vedic mathematics when I was in class 8. I find it very interesting in learning. Gaurav sir made me understand and learnt the art of fast calculations. It is a superb and mind-blowing technique. It has increased the speed of my calculation.

   • Ziya Singh, student, sainthood convent school

1. An ancient methods ofsolving modern mathematics. Wonderful method to boost my calculating ability.

   • Pawan kumar, student, Accurate college

3. I first learnt the art of faster calculation from gaurav sir when I was in school. This technique has changed my calculation ability and speed, and now I can boast of being able to multiply a 5 digit multiplication in my head and that too in 20 seconds.

   • Vansh Rawal, class 7 DSR modern school

4. I got a chance to observe gaurav sir conducting a vedic mathematics class for a teachers. That's when I saw the strength of vedic mathematics. It is a powerful technique to perform swift mental calculations and I suggest that every student be trained in this technique.

   Akash kumar,teacher, holy faith academy